5S: STREAMLINE, STANDARDIZE, SUCCEED. UNLOCK THE POWER OF 5S METHODOLOGY!

THE FIRST STEP TO A SUCCESSFUL OPERATION

DWAYNE FARR

THE FIRST STEP TO A SUCCESSFUL OPERATION INTRODUCES THE 5S METHODOLOGY AND PROVIDES PRACTICAL GUIDANCE ON IMPLEMENTING ITS FIVE KEY PRINCIPLES TO ENHANCE WORKPLACE EFFICIENCY AND PRODUCTIVITY.

The First Step To A Successful Operation

Introduction to 5S Methodology

Historical Context and Origins of 5S

The historical context and origins of the 5S methodology trace back to the evolution of Japanese manufacturing practices. In post-World War II Japan, manufacturers sought to rebuild their industrial infrastructure with a focus on efficiency, quality, and continuous improvement. It was during this period that the principles of 5S began to take shape. The concept of '5S' itself finds its roots in the Japanese words Seiri, Seiton, Seiso, Seiketsu, and Shitsuke, which translate to Sort, Set in Order, Shine, Standardize, and Sustain respectively. These principles were initially espoused by pioneering figures such as Taiichi Ohno and Shigeo Shingo within the Toyota Production System, where they formed the foundation of lean manufacturing. Over time, the 5S methodology gained recognition for its ability to streamline operations, eliminate waste, and enhance workplace organization. By studying the historical context of 5S, we can appreciate how it emerged in response to the specific challenges and aspirations of Japanese manufacturing, ultimately evolving into a globally influential approach for optimizing organizational efficiency. Moreover, understanding the historical origins illuminates the cultural and philosophical underpinnings of 5S, highlighting its emphasis on discipline, teamwork, and continuous improvement. This rich historical perspective provides valuable insights into the enduring relevance and adaptability of 5S across diverse industries and organizational contexts.

Fundamental Concepts and Principles

The chapter of 'Fundamental Concepts and Principles' plays a crucial role in setting the stage for a comprehensive understanding of the 5S methodology. At its core, this section delves into the foundational underpinnings that form the bedrock of 5S, providing readers with an in-depth insight into the principles that shape this paradigm. Central to the concept of 5S is the notion of creating and maintaining a workplace that is not only organized and efficient but also safe and conducive to productivity. This involves systematically addressing issues related to waste, standardized procedures, visual management, and sustained discipline. An in-depth discussion on the significance of each of these components is undertaken, highlighting their interdependence and synergistic effects towards achieving operational excellence. Moreover, by elucidating the fundamental precepts of 5S, readers are empowered with the knowledge and tools necessary for successful application within diverse organizational contexts. From the elimination of unnecessary clutter to the optimization of workflow processes, every facet of 5S is carefully dissected, allowing readers to grasp the holistic nature of this methodology. Additionally, this section explores the theoretical framework underpinning 5S, drawing upon established management principles and methodologies. By connecting 5S to broader management theories, readers gain a robust understanding of its relevance and applicability within contemporary industrial and organizational settings. Furthermore, the importance of fostering a culture of continuous improvement and employee engagement is underscored, emphasizing the participatory nature of 5S implementation. Throughout this section, real-world examples and case studies are utilized to reinforce key concepts, thereby enhancing the practical utility of the content and offering readers actionable insights. Overall, 'Fundamental Concepts and Principles' serves as an intellectual anchor, equipping readers with a firm foundation upon which to build their knowledge and expertise in the realm of 5S methodology.

The Five Pillars of 5S Explained

In the context of workplace organization and efficiency, 5S methodology is often regarded as a foundational framework for improvement. The term '5S' derives from five Japanese words: seiri (sort), seiton (set in order), seiso (shine), seiketsu (standardize), and shitsuke (sustain). These five pillars form the basis of the 5S methodology and serve as guiding principles for creating an optimized work environment.

1. Sort (Seiri): The first pillar, 'Sort', emphasizes the systematic removal of unnecessary items from the work area. This process involves distinguishing between essential and non-essential items, discarding the latter, and organizing the former in a logical manner. By streamlining the work environment, businesses can eliminate clutter and improve overall visibility and accessibility, thereby contributing to heightened productivity.

2. Set in Order (Seiton): Once the unnecessary items have been removed, the next step is to organize and arrange the remaining essential items in a structured manner. This not only facilitates easy access to tools, equipment, and materials but also helps in preventing waste and minimizing the time required to locate essential items. The 'Set in Order' pillar aims to create a visual workplace where everything has a designated place, making it easier to maintain cleanliness and identify abnormalities.

3. Shine (Seiso): Building on the principles of cleanliness and hygiene, the 'Shine' pillar focuses on maintaining a clean and hazard-free working environment. This includes regular cleaning and inspection of the workplace, machinery, and equipment to ensure optimal performance and safety. Through consistent adherence to cleanliness standards, the 'Shine' pillar aims to enhance employee morale, reduce the risk of accidents, and imbue a sense of

discipline and responsibility among workers.

4. Standardize (Seiketsu): Standardization is crucial in sustaining the gains achieved through the previous three pillars. The 'Standardize' pillar involves establishing uniformity in processes, procedures, and methods, as well as implementing visual management tools and checklists to ensure that the workplace remains organized and efficient. By standardizing work practices, businesses can minimize variations, mitigate errors, and facilitate continuous improvement.

5. Sustain (Shitsuke): The final pillar, 'Sustain', focuses on the long-term maintenance of the 5S practices and their integration into the organizational culture. This entails instilling discipline, fostering accountability, and developing a system of checks and audits to sustain the improvements achieved through 5S. By promoting a culture of continuous improvement and employee involvement, the 'Sustain' pillar ensures that the benefits of 5S are perpetually realized and ingrained within the organization's ethos.

Comparative Analysis: 5S vs. Other Methodologies

In comparison to other methodologies focused on workplace organization and efficiency enhancement, the 5S methodology stands out due to its comprehensive approach and sustainable impact. When juxtaposed with traditional methods such as 'clean as you go' or 'red tagging,' 5S proves to be more holistic, addressing not only cleanliness and organization but also standardization, sustainability, and safety. Unlike singularly focused methodologies, 5S encompasses a broader spectrum, emphasizing the importance of maintaining order, ensuring that tools and materials have designated locations, and establishing a standardized approach to daily work processes. This differential aspect reduces waste and minimizes the potential for errors or accidents, distinguishing 5S as a system that creates lasting improvements. Additionally, when compared to Six Sigma or Lean Manufacturing, 5S shines as a foundational framework that lays the groundwork for these more complex methodologies. It serves as a precursor, setting the stage for enhanced problem-solving capabilities and continuous improvement initiatives. The emphasis on sorting, setting in order, shining, standardizing, and sustaining aligns perfectly with the core principles of Lean and Six Sigma, making 5S an essential starting point for organizations aiming to achieve operational excellence. Moreover, unlike certain management approaches that focus solely on short-term gains, 5S fosters a culture of continual improvement, instilling long-lasting habits and behaviors that lead to sustained productivity gains and reduction in safety incidents. As opposed to narrow-focused methods, 5S ensures that the benefits accrued are not short-lived, but enduring. Hence, in the realm of workplace organization and process optimization, the 5S methodology emerges as a comprehensive and foundational framework that underpins and complements other methodologies, contributing significantly to sustainable and holistic improvement.

Strategic Benefits of Implementing 5S

Implementing the 5S methodology within an organization yields a multitude of strategic benefits that significantly impact operational efficiency and overall productivity. One of the key advantages of 5S is the enhancement of workplace safety. By organizing and standardizing the work environment, potential hazards, and risks are minimized, leading to a safer and healthier work atmosphere for employees. Moreover, the systematic arrangement of tools and materials reduces the likelihood of accidents and injuries, contributing to decreased absenteeism and improved employee morale. Additionally, 5S fosters a culture of continuous improvement, enabling teams to identify and rectify inefficiencies promptly. This iterative process not only optimizes processes but also nurtures a culture of proactive problem-solving and innovation. Another strategic benefit of 5S implementation is its contribution to cost reduction. Through the elimination of waste and unnecessary inventory, organizations can realize significant savings in storage costs and material expenses. Furthermore, the streamlined workflow resulting from 5S leads to reduced lead times and enhanced production throughput, ultimately improving the organization's bottom line. Embracing the 5S methodology also augments customer satisfaction by ensuring product quality and on-time delivery. By maintaining a clean and well-organized workplace, companies can uphold high standards of quality and reduce defects, thereby enhancing customer trust and loyalty. Importantly, 5S facilitates a more efficient use of space, optimizing floor layouts and storage areas to maximize utilization. The efficient utilization of space not only enhances productivity but also allows for potential expansion without requiring additional resources. Lastly, 5S plays a crucial role in fostering a culture of accountability and ownership among employees. By involving staff in the process of organizing their workspaces, 5S empowers them to take responsibility for maintaining cleanliness and orderliness, instilling a sense of pride and ownership in their work environment. In conclusion, the strategic benefits of implementing the 5S methodology are far-reaching, encompassing improvements in safety, cost reduction, customer satisfaction, space utilization, and employee engagement, ultimately positioning organizations for sustained success and competitiveness in today's dynamic business environment.

Core Objectives and Expected Outcomes

The core objectives of implementing the 5S methodology are rooted in achieving operational excellence, enhancing workplace organization, and optimizing efficiency. By systematically integrating the principles of Sort, Set in Order, Shine, Standardize, and Sustain, organizations aim to create an environment that promotes safety, productivity, and quality. This structured approach facilitates the elimination of waste, reduction of downtime, and overall improvement in workflow processes.

Furthermore, the expected outcomes of embracing 5S extend beyond mere physical tidiness. Through the meticulous arrangement of tools, equipment, and materials, the methodology strives to foster a culture of discipline, responsibility, and continuous improvement among employees. As a result, businesses anticipate heightened employee morale, reduced error rates, and enhanced product or service quality.

Moreover, the implementation of 5S is intrinsically linked to cost savings and resource optimization. By streamlining workstations, storage areas, and production lines, organizations can minimize excess inventory, decrease lead times, and maximize space utilization. This not only reduces operational costs but also contributes to a more sustainable approach to resource management.

In addition to these benefits, another critical outcome of employing 5S is the creation of a visual workplace. The use of color coding, labeling, and signage not only enhances efficiency in locating items but also communicates standards and procedures effectively. This visual management aspect promotes transparency, streamlined communication, and improved adherence to best practices throughout the organization.

Finally, it's important to recognize that the impact of 5S implementation goes beyond the shop floor. By instilling a culture of continuous improvement and efficiency, organizations can enhance their overall strategic positioning, customer satisfaction, and competitive advantage in the market. Therefore, the core objectives and expected outcomes of 5S are deeply interconnected with operational, cultural, and financial facets of organizational performance.

Industry Applications and Scope

In the realm of industrial methodologies, the 5S system has garnered widespread attention for its versatile applications across various sectors. The scope of 5S implementation extends far beyond traditional manufacturing settings and is increasingly relevant in service-based industries, healthcare facilities, offices, and even educational institutions. The fundamental principles of Sort, Set in Order, Shine, Standardize, and Sustain are universally adaptable, allowing organizations to streamline processes and enhance operational efficiency irrespective of their specific industry. This adaptability has led to the integration of 5S practices in automotive manufacturing plants, pharmaceutical companies, food processing units, and logistics and distribution centers.

One notable industry where 5S has displayed remarkable efficacy is healthcare. The meticulous organization and cleanliness inherent in the 5S philosophy are particularly beneficial in clinical settings, where patient safety and infection control are paramount. Implementation of 5S in hospitals and clinics has led to reduced medical errors, improved staff productivity, and enhanced patient satisfaction. Moreover, 5S methodologies have proven instrumental in minimizing waste and optimizing workflow in hospital environments.

The financial sector also stands to gain considerable advantages from 5S adoption. By applying the 5S principles, such as eliminating clutter and standardizing processes, financial institutions can optimize their workspace layout and reduce operational inefficiencies. This approach paves the way for a more structured and compliant environment, fostering smoother customer interactions and bolstering overall service quality.

When considering the scope of 5S within educational institutions, the benefits become evident. With the burgeoning emphasis on student-centered learning and collaborative teaching methods, maintaining an organized and conducive learning environment is pivotal. By incorporating 5S practices into school operations, educational institutions can cultivate an atmosphere that promotes focus, creativity, and safety among students and educators. Through standardized storage solutions and regular cleaning schedules, schools can create an environment that supports effective learning and teaching experiences.

The scope of 5S methodology is not limited by industry boundaries but encompasses a wide array of sectors, each reaping its rewards through disciplined organization, standardized processes, and sustained improvements. As the 5S framework continues to evolve, its potential for enhancing workplace functionalities across diverse industries remains robust, making it an indispensable tool for organizations striving for operational excellence.

Key Success Factors for 5S Implementation

In order to ensure a successful implementation of the 5S methodology, it is crucial to understand the key success factors that contribute to its effectiveness. First and foremost, commitment from top management is essential. Without the explicit support and involvement of leadership, the implementation of 5S is unlikely to gain traction across the organization. Leadership should not only endorse the initiative but also actively participate in its execution, demonstrating a clear alignment with the 5S principles.

Another critical success factor is employee engagement. The buy-in and active participation of all employees at every level are pivotal for the sustained success of 5S. This requires comprehensive training and communication to instill an understanding of the benefits and practical application of 5S in their daily work. Moreover, creating a culture that encourages and rewards continuous improvement and adherence to 5S principles is imperative to drive lasting change.

Effective resource allocation is also a key consideration. Adequate resources, both in terms of time and budget, must be allocated to support the implementation of 5S. This includes providing necessary tools, equipment, and infrastructure to facilitate the sorting, organizing, cleaning, standardizing, and sustaining efforts integral to the 5S methodology.

Furthermore, clear and measurable objectives are essential for guiding the implementation process. Setting specific targets and key performance indicators allows the organization to track progress, identify areas for improvement, and celebrate achievements. Regular audits and reviews play a pivotal role in monitoring the ongoing effectiveness of 5S practices and identifying opportunities for refinement.

Lastly, fostering a spirit of continuous improvement is critical. The 5S journey does not culminate once the initial implementation phase is complete; rather, it necessitates an ongoing commitment to sustaining and enhancing the 5S standards. Encouraging feedback from employees, learning from setbacks, and adapting to evolving business needs are fundamental aspects of maintaining the momentum of 5S. By prioritizing these key success factors, organizations can lay a solid foundation for the successful adoption and integration of 5S into their operational ethos.

Role of Leadership in Facilitating 5S

Effective leadership is integral to the successful implementation of the 5S methodology within an organization. Leaders play a pivotal role in cultivating a culture of continuous improvement and operational excellence, both of which are central tenets of 5S. This section will delve into the multifaceted responsibilities and strategies that leaders must embrace to ensure the seamless integration of 5S principles into the organizational fabric.

At the outset, leaders need to champion the 5S initiative, fostering buy-in across all levels of the organization. This entails clearly communicating the rationale behind 5S, its potential benefits, and the expected impact on day-to-day operations. By articulating a compelling vision for 5S, leaders can inspire commitment and enthusiasm among employees, paving the way for sustained engagement throughout the implementation process.

Moreover, leaders are tasked with allocating resources and establishing clear accountability structures to support 5S initiatives. They must ensure that the necessary tools, training, and infrastructure are readily available to enable employees to seamlessly adopt 5S practices. Additionally, leaders should designate cross-functional teams and assign specific roles to individuals, thereby fostering a sense of ownership and responsibility for 5S outcomes.

In facilitating 5S, leaders must lead by example, embodying the principles they advocate. Through active participation in 5S activities and adherence to established standards, leaders demonstrate their commitment to the cause, setting a precedent for others to follow. Furthermore, they should provide continuous feedback and recognition to reinforce desired behaviors and motivate sustained adherence to 5S protocols.

Beyond these aspects, effective leadership involves nurturing a culture of continuous improvement, wherein employees feel empowered to identify and address inefficiencies in their workspaces. Leaders should encourage open communication and solicitation of ideas, ensuring that employees feel valued as active contributors to the 5S journey. Additionally, leaders play a crucial role in cultivating resilience and perseverance, acknowledging that the path to sustained 5S excellence may present challenges, yet remaining steadfast in their commitment to the vision.

In summary, the role of leadership in facilitating 5S is multi-faceted, encompassing visionary communication, resource allocation, active participation, reinforcement of behaviors, and the cultivation of an empowered and resilient workforce. When leaders embrace these responsibilities with dedication and conviction, they pave the way for a transformational journey towards operational excellence and organizational efficiency.

Summary and Precursor to 'Sort'

The role of leadership in facilitating 5S is crucial for the successful implementation and sustenance of the methodology within an organization. As discussed in the previous section, effective leadership provides the necessary guidance, support, and resources to drive a cultural shift towards 5S principles. However, before diving into the specific phases of 5S, it is imperative to comprehend the overarching significance of the methodology and lay the groundwork for its practical application. This section serves as a comprehensive summary of the key tenets outlined in the preceding chapters while also setting the stage for the initial phase of 5S, known as 'Sort.' Reflecting on the historical context and origins of 5S, we recognize its roots in Japanese management techniques, particularly in the Toyota Production System. Understanding these origins offers insight into the evolution and refinement of 5S as a systematic approach to optimizing workplace efficiency. The fundamental concepts and principles underpinning 5S highlight its emphasis on organization, cleanliness, standardization, and sustainability. By delving into the five pillars of 5S - Sort, Set in Order, Shine, Standardize, and Sustain - individuals gain a deeper understanding of the interconnected stages that form the foundation of this methodology. Additionally, through a comparative analysis with other management methodologies, such as Kaizen and Lean Manufacturing, the unique value proposition of 5S becomes apparent, showcasing its holistic nature in addressing organizational challenges. Strategic benefits, including improved productivity, safety enhancements, waste reduction, and employee satisfaction, underscore the compelling reasons for adopting 5S practices in diverse operational contexts. Establishing core objectives and anticipated outcomes delineates the intended impact of 5S implementation, directing attention towards achieving measurable improvements across various facets of the business. Furthermore, exploring industry applications and scope elucidates the versatility of 5S, demonstrating its relevance across manufacturing, healthcare, services, and beyond. While acknowledging the critical role of leadership in enabling 5S, identifying key success factors and emphasizing the involvement of all levels of the organization reinforces the collective responsibility embedded within the 5S framework. Finally, this section culminates in a seamless transition to the next chapter, laying the groundwork for 'Sort' by encapsulating the preparatory insights essential for embarking on the first step of 5S implementation.

The First Step To A Successful Operation

Understanding the Importance of 'Sort'

Defining 'Sort' in the 5S Context

The 'Sort' phase is a fundamental aspect of the 5S methodology, playing a crucial role in organizing the work environment for maximum efficiency. This pivotal step involves the systematic identification and segregation of necessary items from unnecessary items, thereby paving the way for a clutter-free workplace. By meticulously categorizing items based on their relevance to the operational processes, organizations can significantly enhance productivity and workflow consistency.

In the context of 5S, the 'Sort' phase encompasses far more than physical tidying. It fosters a mindset shift towards prioritizing essential tools, materials, and equipment necessary for daily operations while mitigating the hindrances posed by surplus or redundant items. Understanding the core principles of 'Sort' is integral to the successful implementation of the entire 5S framework, as it lays the groundwork for subsequent stages such as 'Set in Order', 'Shine', 'Standardize', and 'Sustain'.

One of the primary objectives of the 'Sort' phase is to identify clutter within the workspace and recognize its direct correlation with diminished operational effectiveness. Clutter, whether tangible or intangible, can impede workflow, increase the likelihood of errors, and impact employee morale. By acknowledging the detrimental impact of clutter, organizations can proactively address these challenges through the structured sorting process.

Moreover, 'Sort' serves as a catalyst for refining inventory management practices by distinguishing between vital items that actively contribute to operational processes and those that are redundant or obsolete. This delineation not only streamlines the retrieval of essential tools but also optimizes storage space, reduces inventory costs, and minimizes the risk of misplaced items. Effective sorting expedites inventory audits and contributes to the development of leaner, more efficient supply chains.

Beyond its material implications, the 'Sort' phase instills a mentality of continuous improvement by encouraging employees to critically evaluate their workspaces and practices. Through this introspective lens, individuals gain insight into the impact of organizational efficiency and are empowered to contribute to an environment conducive to sustained productivity. Moreover, fostering a culture of 'Sort' encourages employees to exercise discernment in their decision-making, thereby promoting accountability and conscientiousness across all operational facets.

Ultimately, the 'Sort' phase forms the bedrock upon which the overarching goals of the 5S methodology rest. By aligning the organization's resources with its operational needs, 'Sort' sets the stage for the seamless integration of subsequent 5S phases and sets the tone for sustained and impactful transformation.

Identifying Clutter and Its Impact on Efficiency

Clutter within a workspace is often insidious, accumulating gradually over time and becoming so familiar that its negative impact on efficiency can go unnoticed. However, the adverse effects of clutter are far-reaching and detrimental to operational excellence. Understanding the impact of clutter is essential in the 5S methodology as it forms the foundation for the 'Sort' phase. By recognizing and addressing clutter, organizations can pave the way for a more streamlined and productive work environment.

One of the primary consequences of clutter is the hindrance it poses to productivity and workflow. When unnecessary items, tools, or materials are scattered throughout the workspace, employees may expend valuable time searching for what they need, disrupting the flow of work and contributing to delays. Furthermore, clutter creates visual distractions, increasing mental fatigue and reducing focus, leading to errors and rework. In essence, clutter acts as a silent disruptor, sapping energy and efficiency from the workforce.

Moreover, clutter can impede safety within the workplace. Excessive items stored haphazardly can create tripping hazards, obstruct emergency exits, or contribute to accidents. This not only jeopardizes the well-being of employees but also introduces potential liabilities for the organization. Therefore, identifying clutter and its potential risks is crucial for maintaining a safe and compliant working environment.

In addition to its impact on productivity and safety, clutter can also have financial implications for an organization. Unused or duplicate inventory takes up valuable space, increasing storage costs and reducing available working areas. Furthermore, the accumulation of obsolete equipment or materials ties up capital that could be invested more lucratively elsewhere. Recognizing the financial toll of clutter prompts organizations to prioritize the 'Sort' phase, making informed decisions about what is truly necessary and valuable to the operation.

Finally, clutter can significantly affect employee morale and motivation. A disorganized and cluttered workspace can give the impression of chaos and inefficiency, impacting the overall perception of job satisfaction and pride in work. By tackling clutter, organizations demonstrate a commitment to providing a conducive and supportive environment for their employees, which can foster a positive culture and heightened engagement.

By understanding the multifaceted impact of clutter on efficiency, organizations can underscore the importance of the 'Sort' phase in the 5S methodology, laying the groundwork for transformative change in the work environment.

Criteria for Sorting: What to Keep

When implementing the 'Sort' stage of the 5S methodology, determining what to keep is a critical aspect of the process. Efficiently identifying and categorizing items based on specific criteria not only facilitates a clutter-free work environment but also contributes to improved productivity and safety within the workplace. The following criteria serve as guidelines for effectively determining what items should be retained:

1. Frequency of Use: Items that are frequently used in daily operations should be readily accessible and remain in close proximity to the workstation. This criterion helps optimize workflow and reduces time spent searching for essential tools or materials.

2. Value and Purpose: Assessing the value and purpose of each item is crucial in deciding whether it warrants inclusion in the workspace. Items that directly contribute to production, quality, or safety should be prioritized over those that serve minimal or obsolete functions.

3. Safety and Compliance: Items that align with safety regulations and compliance standards must be retained to ensure a secure working environment. Additionally, non-compliant or hazardous materials should be carefully segregated or disposed of according to established protocols.

4. Seasonal or Project-Based Needs: Some items may have utility during specific seasons or projects. It is essential to determine whether these items are genuinely necessary for ongoing operations or if their usage is limited to temporary, situational requirements.

5. Future Need and Historical Significance: Evaluating the potential future need or historical significance of items can aid in decision-making. Identifying relevant historical data or forecasting future requirements helps prevent unnecessary disposal of potentially valuable assets.

6. Space Optimization: Items that consume excessive space without contributing significantly to operational efficiency should be subject to thorough assessment. Optimizing spatial utilization ensures a more organized and visually appealing workspace.

7. Redundancy and Duplication: Identifying and rectifying redundant or duplicated items is crucial to prevent unnecessary stockpiling. Eliminating duplicates reduces inventory costs and minimizes confusion regarding item location.

By applying these criteria, organizations can systematically evaluate and decide which items merit retention within their workspaces. Adhering to these guidelines ensures that the 'Sort' phase of the 5S process is conducted with precision and forethought, ultimately leading to a streamlined and productive workplace.

Tools and Techniques for Effective Sorting

In the pursuit of operational excellence, the process of sorting is elevated by the application of robust tools and techniques. These aids serve to streamline the sorting process, ensuring a more efficient and effective outcome. One such tool is the 5S Red Tag strategy, which involves tagging items that are deemed unnecessary or unused in the immediate work area. This visual tagging system serves as a catalyst for identifying and ultimately removing non-essential items. Furthermore, the systematic use of checklists can significantly enhance the sorting process. By providing clear criteria and guidelines, checklists empower employees to make informed decisions about what should stay and what should go, thereby minimizing ambiguity and subjectivity. Additionally, the implementation of designated sorting zones within the workspace can greatly facilitate the sorting process. These zones, such as 'keep', 'sell/donate', 'discard', and 'relocate', ensure that items undergoing assessment have a clear path towards their respective dispositions. Another valuable technique is the 5 Whys method, a problem-solving tool that delves into the root causes of clutter and excess. By repeatedly asking 'why' an item is present or why a certain practice exists, employees can uncover deeper issues that contribute to unnecessary accumulation. Pairing this with visual management tools such as shadow boards and floor markings further reinforces the sorting process, ensuring that items are returned to their designated locations after use. Moreover, the practice of standardizing the sorting process through well-documented procedures and training materials can institutionalize best practices, enabling consistency across different areas of the organization. Embracing digital solutions like inventory management software can also revolutionize the sorting process, providing real-time visibility into the status and location of items, thereby aiding in decision-making regarding their disposition. Lastly, embracing Kaizen events dedicated to sorting can serve as a focused platform for driving continuous improvement and instilling a culture of efficiency. The integration of these tools and techniques not only accelerates the sorting process but also fosters a sustainable culture of tidiness and orderliness within the workplace, ultimately contributing to enhanced productivity and resource optimization.

The Cost Implications of Excess and Waste

Excess and waste within the workplace can have far-reaching implications for an organization, impacting its bottom line and overall operational efficiency. When resources, whether it be time, materials, or space, are misallocated or underutilized, the costs incurred can quickly accumulate and impede productivity. In the context of the 5S methodology, the 'Sort' phase highlights the need to identify and address these cost implications head-on.

One significant aspect of excess and waste is the financial burden it places on a company. When unnecessary items clutter the workspace, valuable time is expended in searching for required tools, equipment, or documents, leading to a direct impact on labor costs. Furthermore, excess inventory ties up capital and incurs carrying costs such as storage, handling, and potential obsolescence, impacting the balance sheet.

In addition to direct financial costs, there are also indirect implications that arise from excess and waste. The inefficiencies resulting from disorganization and clutter can lead to errors, rework, and delays in production, further magnifying the costs associated with poor sorting practices. Moreover, excessive waste can strain environmental resources and contribute to a negative ecological footprint, aligning poorly with sustainable business practices.

To counter these cost implications, organizations must strategically address excess and waste through proper sorting and elimination of non-essential items. By doing so, they can achieve cost savings through reduced inventory, improved workflows, and minimized downtime. Additionally, the effective management of waste promotes a cleaner, safer work environment, which can positively influence employee morale and overall job satisfaction.

It is imperative to recognize that the cost implications of excess and waste extend beyond immediate financial constraints and encompass broader impacts on an organization's competitiveness, reputation, and long-term sustainability. Incorporating a mindset of waste reduction and cost-consciousness during the 'Sort' phase of 5S is therefore pivotal in ensuring a leaner, more efficient, and ultimately more successful operation.

Developing a Culture of Continuous Sorting

In order to fully embrace the principles of 'Sort' within the 5S methodology, organizations must strive to develop a culture of continuous sorting. This entails ingraining the habit of regular assessment and removal of unnecessary items into the daily operations and mindset of all employees. By fostering a workplace environment where sorting is seen as an ongoing process rather than a one-time event, companies can consistently maintain organized and efficient workspaces.

Key to this cultural shift is the establishment of clear guidelines and expectations regarding sorting responsibilities. Leadership should communicate the importance of sorting as a fundamental practice that contributes to overall productivity and waste reduction. Employees at all levels should be encouraged to take ownership of their immediate work areas and actively participate in the sorting process. Furthermore, providing training and resources to support staff in identifying and addressing clutter can significantly contribute to the success of continuous sorting initiatives.

Additionally, integrating sorting activities into the regular workflow through structured routines and schedules can help embed the practice into the organizational DNA. Whether through daily mini-sorting sessions or weekly designated sorting time, creating dedicated slots for sorting activities ensures that it becomes a consistent part of the operational cadence. Effective visual management tools can aid in this process by providing clear indicators and reminders for employees to engage in sorting exercises. Moreover, recognizing and celebrating achievements in maintaining clean and organized spaces can serve as positive reinforcement for sustaining the culture of continuous sorting.

Organizations that successfully develop a culture of continuous sorting stand to benefit from enhanced operational efficiency, reduced waste, and improved workplace safety. Embracing this proactive approach to organization lays the foundation for the subsequent stages of the 5S methodology, setting the stage for sustainable improvements in overall workplace functionality and cleanliness.

Training Staff for Successful Sorting Initiatives

Effective training is a cornerstone of successful sorting initiatives within the 5S methodology. As organizations strive to optimize their workspaces and processes, it becomes essential to equip employees with the knowledge and skills required to execute sorting activities with precision and proficiency. Training staff for successful sorting initiatives involves a comprehensive approach that encompasses both theoretical understanding and practical application.

To begin with, training programs should educate employees about the principles of 'Sort' in the context of 5S. This includes imparting an understanding of the significance of decluttering and organizing the workspace to eliminate waste and streamline operations. Employees should be familiarized with the criteria and decision-making processes involved in determining what items are essential and conducive to a well-organized workspace.

Furthermore, hands-on training is crucial for enabling staff to effectively implement the sorting process. Practical sessions can involve interactive workshops where employees actively categorize and organize items in the workplace, applying the principles they have learned. Additionally, providing guidance on the utilization of specific tools and techniques for sorting, such as red tagging and visual labels, can empower employees to make informed decisions during the sorting process.

In tandem with this, it is imperative to instill a sense of ownership and responsibility among employees regarding the sorting initiatives. Training should emphasize the individual and collective roles in sustaining a clutter-free environment and continuously improving the organization's operational efficiency. This may involve instilling a mindset of continuous improvement and fostering a culture where every employee takes pride in contributing to a clean and organized workspace.

Moreover, incorporating real-world examples and case studies into the training curriculum can offer insights into successful sorting initiatives in similar organizational settings. By examining these examples, employees can gain valuable perspectives on the practical application of sorting principles and understand the positive impact of effective sorting on the overall work environment and productivity.

Additionally, ongoing support and reinforcement are essential components of training staff for successful sorting initiatives. Regular check-ins, refresher courses, and open channels for feedback and suggestions can aid in sustaining the momentum of sorting initiatives and addressing any challenges or concerns that may arise.

Overall, effective training for sorting initiatives is an investment in the organization's operational excellence. It equips employees with the knowledge, skills, and motivation necessary to embrace the principles of 'Sort' and contribute proactively to the creation of an efficient, organized, and productive workspace.

Visual Management Tools for Sorting Success

In the context of implementing the 5S methodology, visual management tools play a fundamental role in ensuring the success of the 'Sort' phase. These tools are essential for creating an organized and visually intuitive workplace that supports efficient sorting activities. Visual management tools leverage visual cues to communicate information clearly and effectively, aiding in the identification of items, defining storage locations, and demonstrating process flows. In this section, we explore the key elements of visual management tools for sorting success.

One of the primary visual management tools used in sorting is color coding. Color coding allows for the categorization of items based on specific criteria, such as frequency of use, item type, or production stage. By assigning distinct colors to different categories, employees can easily identify and sort items, reducing the risk of errors and confusion. Additionally, color coding contributes to maintaining the designated places for items, supporting the 'Set in Order' phase of 5S.

Another vital visual management tool is shadow boards or outlines. These tools involve creating outlines or silhouettes of tools or equipment on boards or workstations, indicating where each item should be placed after use. Shadow boards not only provide a clear visual reference for item placement but also enable swift identification of missing items, prompting immediate corrective action. As a result, this promotes tidiness and enhances workplace organization.

Furthermore, signage and labeling are crucial visual management tools that aid in sorting. Clear and concise signage helps in guiding employees to the correct locations for storing items, while well-designed labels contribute to easy identification and retrieval of items during sorting processes. When applied consistently, effective signage and labeling can significantly reduce the time spent searching for items, leading to productivity gains and streamlined operations.

Visual scoreboards and performance dashboards are also valuable tools for sorting success. These displays provide real-time visual indicators of progress and performance, showcasing sorting metrics, targets, and key performance indicators (KPIs). By making sorting metrics transparent and accessible, visual scoreboards motivate employees to adhere to sorting standards and drive continuous improvement initiatives.

Finally, visual management tools encompass the use of floor markings and tape, which define pathways, storage areas, and work zones. These markings visually delineate designated areas for sorting activities, preventing clutter and congestion. Additionally, floor markings aid in sustaining the benefits of sorting by reinforcing spatial organization and safety practices.

The effective deployment of these visual management tools not only supports the 'Sort' phase but also sets the foundation for subsequent stages of the 5S methodology, contributing to sustained organizational efficiency and a culture of continuous improvement.

Real-World Examples of Effective Sorting

In the realm of operational efficiency, real-world examples serve as compelling evidence of the efficacy of sorting processes in various industries. One such example is the implementation of 5S by a leading automotive manufacturing company. By meticulously sorting through their production line, they were able to eliminate unnecessary tools and equipment, resulting in reduced setup times and increased productivity. Similarly, a large-scale warehousing facility undertook a comprehensive sorting initiative, categorizing their inventory and optimizing storage space. As a result, they experienced a significant reduction in picking errors and an overall improvement in order fulfillment accuracy.

Moving beyond the realm of traditional manufacturing, healthcare organizations have also leveraged sorting principles to streamline their operations. A notable case study involves a hospital that introduced a systematic approach to sorting medical supplies and equipment. This led to a reduction in patient wait times and an enhanced ability to respond swiftly to emergencies, ultimately improving patient care and staff satisfaction.

Furthermore, in the realm of service industries, a major telecommunications company successfully applied 5S sorting principles to their customer service operations. By eliminating redundant documentation and organizing workstations systematically, they were able to enhance their response times and uphold service quality standards, thereby improving customer satisfaction metrics.

Small and medium-sized enterprises (SMEs) have also reaped the benefits of effective sorting. A local precision engineering firm achieved remarkable results by implementing a tailored 5S sorting strategy. This involved decluttering workstations, organizing tools, and establishing visual cues for item placement, leading to a reduction in production lead times and an increase in overall workplace safety.

These diverse examples underscore the universal applicability and profound impact of sorting processes. They demonstrate that irrespective of the industry or organizational size, adopting a structured approach to sorting not only enhances operational efficiency but also creates a conducive environment for continuous improvement.

Evaluating the Outcomes of the Sorting Process

Evaluating the outcomes of the sorting process is a critical step in the 5S methodology. It allows organizations to assess the effectiveness of their sorting initiatives and determine the impact on overall efficiency and productivity. By conducting a thorough evaluation, companies can identify areas of improvement, celebrate successes, and make data-driven decisions for future sorting efforts.

One key aspect of evaluating the outcomes of the sorting process is measuring the reduction in waste and clutter within the workspace. This can be quantified through metrics such as reduced inventory levels, minimized storage space requirements, and decreased material handling times. By establishing baseline measurements before the sorting process and comparing them with post-sorting data, organizations can quantify the tangible benefits of sorting.

In addition to quantitative measures, it is essential to consider qualitative factors when evaluating the sorting outcomes. This includes assessing employee satisfaction and engagement, as well as the overall visual appeal and tidiness of the workplace. A well-sorted and organized environment not only improves operational efficiency but also contributes to a positive work culture and employee morale.

Moreover, evaluating the outcomes of the sorting process involves gathering feedback from employees at all levels of the organization. Their insights and observations provide valuable perspectives on the impact of sorting on day-to-day operations and can reveal opportunities for further enhancements. Employee feedback sessions, surveys, or focus groups can be instrumental in capturing qualitative data that complements the quantitative evaluation of sorting outcomes.

Furthermore, conducting an assessment of the financial implications of the sorting process is crucial. This involves analyzing cost savings achieved through reduced waste, optimized space utilization, and streamlined processes. By calculating the return on investment (ROI) of sorting initiatives, organizations can justify the resources allocated to the 5S methodology and garner support for future improvement projects.

Another vital aspect of evaluating sorting outcomes is benchmarking against industry standards and best practices. This comparative analysis can provide valuable insights into where the organization stands in terms of operational excellence and identify opportunities for further advancement. Learning from the success stories of other companies and adapting proven strategies can accelerate the continuous improvement journey.

In summary, evaluating the outcomes of the sorting process encompasses both quantitative and qualitative assessments, employee feedback, financial analysis, and benchmarking activities. It serves as a foundation for ongoing improvement efforts and reinforces the principles of 5S as a sustainable approach to organizational excellence.

The First Step To A Successful Operation

'Set in Order': Creating a Systematic Workspace

Introduction to 'Set in Order'

Establishing a systematic workspace forms the bedrock of operational proficiency and overall organizational effectiveness. Through meticulous organization and arrangement, businesses can optimize their resources, enhance productivity, and streamline their workflows with greater efficiency. The principles of 'Set in Order' advance beyond mere tidiness, emphasizing the strategic placement of tools, materials, and equipment to eliminate waste, minimize time wastage, and reduce errors. A systematically arranged workspace not only accelerates task completion but also contributes to a safer and more engaging work environment, fostering employee satisfaction and morale. By implementing the principles of 'Set in Order,' businesses can harness the full potential of their operations, propelling them towards sustainable success and competitive edge. Embracing order within the workspace transcends cleanliness; it transcends a mere visual appeal. It lays the foundation for logic, structure, and harmony within the workplace, enabling employees to navigate effortlessly through their tasks without needless obstructions. When all elements are organized in their rightful place, the workforce experiences heightened clarity, reduced frustration, and a sense of control over their domain. Furthermore, by standardizing the arrangement of items, a company cultivates an environment where operations can seamlessly progress, unimpeded by disorder or inefficiency. The criticality of setting things in order extends across industries and sectors, underscoring its universal applicability in optimizing operational processes and performance. Whether in manufacturing, healthcare, hospitality, or administrative domains, an organized workspace serves as the cornerstone for achieving desired outcomes effectively and consistently. As we delve deeper into the intricacies of 'Set in Order,' it becomes palpable that the pursuit of orderliness is integral to the ethos of any high-functioning enterprise. Therefore, understanding, embracing, and effectively implementing the principles of 'Set in Order' stands as a pivotal determinant of an organization's ability to harmonize its various functions and achieve operational excellence.

Principles of Effective Organization

Achieving a well-organized workspace is pivotal in enhancing operational efficiency and productivity. Principles of effective organization set the foundation for an environment where workflow is uninterrupted, tools are readily accessible, and safety concerns are minimized. Understanding and implementing these principles can lead to a workspace that not only looks organized but also functions seamlessly.

One fundamental principle is the concept of visual management, which involves utilizing visual cues such as color coding, labels, and signage to quickly convey information about tools, materials, and processes. This not only aids in finding items efficiently but also helps in maintaining order by clearly indicating where items belong. Additionally, visual management contributes to error reduction and standardization, as it minimizes the chances of misplaced items or incorrect tool usage.

Another key principle is ergonomic organization, ensuring that tools and materials are arranged in a manner that reduces physical strain on workers while promoting efficient access. This involves considering factors such as frequency of use, weight and size of items, and the natural movement of employees within the workspace. By applying ergonomic principles to workspace organization, businesses can mitigate the risk of workplace injuries and enhance employee comfort and productivity.

Furthermore, the principle of standardization plays a vital role in effective organization. Establishing standardized locations for tools and materials streamlines processes and reduces the potential for confusion or mistakes. Consistency in storage and arrangement facilitates smooth operations and equips employees with a clear understanding of where to find the necessary resources.

An often overlooked yet critical principle is the concept of continuous improvement. Organizational systems should be agile enough to adapt to changing needs and challenges. Regular reviews and refinements based on feedback from employees and observations of workflow patterns enable organizations to continuously optimize their organizational setup. Embracing a culture of continuous improvement ensures that the workspace remains responsive to evolving demands, ultimately bolstering overall efficiency.

In conclusion, the principles of effective organization form the backbone of a systematic and efficient workspace. Employing visual management, ergonomic considerations, standardization, and a focus on continuous improvement lays the groundwork for a workspace that fosters productivity, safety, and employee satisfaction.

Identifying Key Tools and Materials

In the pursuit of creating a systematic workspace, it is crucial to identify and understand the key tools and materials that are integral to the operational processes within the workspace. This entails a comprehensive analysis of all tools, equipment, and materials used in the day-to-day activities. By gaining a clear understanding of these elements, organizations can streamline their processes, reduce waste, and enhance efficiency. Start by conducting an inventory of all tools and materials present in the workspace. This inventory should encompass everything from machinery and equipment to smaller hand tools and supplies. Having a centralized database or system to track and manage these items can be immensely beneficial in this regard. Once the inventory is established, categorize the tools and materials based on their frequency of use, criticality to operations, and storage requirements. This categorization allows for a more organized approach to managing and storing these items. Additionally, it enables the identification of redundant or obsolete tools and materials that can be eliminated or replaced, further optimizing the workspace. Collaborate with personnel who are directly involved in utilizing these tools and materials. Their insights and feedback can provide valuable information regarding the practicality and efficiency of the existing tools and materials. Furthermore, involving employees in this process fosters a sense of ownership and encourages accountability in maintaining the organized workspace. Through this collaborative effort, you can harness the collective expertise and experience of your workforce to make informed decisions about the tools and materials necessary for a systematic and efficient workspace. In conclusion, identifying key tools and materials is a fundamental step in the journey towards creating a systematic workspace. It involves thorough inventory management, categorization based on usage and importance, and active involvement of personnel. By diligently undertaking this process, organizations can lay a solid foundation for the implementation of 'Set in Order' principles, leading to enhanced productivity and operational excellence.

Creating an Efficient Layout

Efficient layout design is crucial for optimizing workflow and productivity within the workspace. A well-planned layout enables easy access to tools and materials, minimizes movement time, and enhances overall operational effectiveness. When creating an efficient layout, it is essential to consider various aspects that contribute to a streamlined and organized workspace.

Firstly, analyzing the workflow and process requirements is imperative. Understanding how different tasks are interconnected and identifying key work zones can help in determining the most effective layout. By mapping out the flow of activities and considering the frequency of tool and material usage, one can strategically position workstations and storage areas to minimize unnecessary movements.

Moreover, ergonomic considerations play a vital role in layout design. Ensuring that workstations are designed to promote proper posture and reduce physical strain can significantly impact employee comfort and efficiency. This involves adjusting the height of work surfaces, providing adequate lighting, and creating clear pathways to prevent obstructions.

Another important aspect of creating an efficient layout is the allocation of space. Utilizing available space optimally while avoiding clutter is essential. Careful consideration should be given to the placement of equipment, machinery, and storage units to maximize usable space without compromising safety and accessibility.

Additionally, the implementation of visual cues such as floor markings, color-coded zones, and shadow boards can aid in guiding employees to specific areas and maintaining the organized layout. These visual aids can also support the standardization of processes, contributing to a consistent and efficient operational environment.

Incorporating input from employees who directly engage with the workspace is invaluable when designing an efficient layout. Their insights can provide practical perspectives on improving the arrangement of tools and materials based on their daily tasks and responsibilities. Furthermore, involving employees in the layout design fosters a sense of ownership and encourages adherence to the established organizational system.

Ultimately, creating an efficient layout requires a balance between functionality, safety, and employee comfort. It is an ongoing process that may necessitate periodic reassessment and adjustments to align with evolving operational needs and best practices.

Labeling and Signage Best Practices

In any workplace, labeling and signage play a crucial role in maintaining a systematic and well-organized environment. Clear and effective labeling of tools, equipment, materials, and workspace areas is essential for improving operational efficiency, safety, and overall productivity.

When implementing labeling and signage best practices, it's important to consider the following key aspects:

1. Consistency and Standardization: Establishing consistent labeling formats and standards across all areas of the workspace ensures that employees can easily locate items and understand important information at a glance. Standardized color-coding systems for different categories of items can further enhance clarity and organization.

2. Clarity and Readability: Labels and signs should be clear, legible, and easily understandable from a distance. Using large fonts, high-contrast colors, and simple, universally recognized symbols can significantly improve the visibility and comprehension of important information.

3. Location-Specific Signage: Tailoring signage to specific areas within the workspace is

crucial for providing contextually relevant information. This may include directional signs, hazard warnings, operating instructions, and safety guidelines placed in strategic locations to guide and inform employees as they navigate the workspace.

4. Safety and Regulatory Compliance: Ensuring that all labeling and signage align with industry regulations and safety standards is paramount. Properly labeled hazardous materials, emergency exits, fire extinguisher locations, and other safety-related information contribute to a secure and compliant working environment.

5. Maintenance and Review: Regular inspection and maintenance of labels and signage are necessary to prevent deterioration, fading, or loss of clarity over time. Periodic reviews of the effectiveness and relevance of existing labels and signs should be conducted to identify areas for improvement.

By prioritizing labeling and signage best practices, organizations can streamline workflow, minimize errors, reduce the risk of workplace accidents, and foster a culture of order and accountability. Effective communication through visual cues and clear identification supports the fundamental principles of 'Set in Order' and significantly contributes to the success of the 5S methodology.

Utilizing Visual Controls for Workflow Enhancement

Visual controls play a crucial role in enhancing workflow efficiency and maintaining systematic order in the workplace. By implementing visual cues such as color-coded labels, floor markings, and signage, organizations can significantly improve their operational processes. These visual tools serve as powerful aids in guiding employees through tasks, reducing errors, and streamlining overall operations. Furthermore, they contribute to a safer work environment by clearly demarcating hazardous areas or indicating safety protocols. Visual controls not only facilitate smooth workflow but also support continuous improvement efforts within the organization. When properly designed and strategically placed, these visual indicators provide a standardized, easily understandable system that fosters consistency across different work areas. This aids in reducing confusion and minimizing the risk of mistakes. Additionally, visual controls support the 5S methodology's 'Set in Order' principle, as they help create a visually organized workspace where everything has its place. They enable workers to quickly identify tools, materials, and equipment, leading to time savings and improved productivity. Moreover, by leveraging visual controls, companies can ensure compliance with regulatory standards and industry best practices, ultimately boosting their reputation and trustworthiness. When considering the broader impact, visual controls also contribute to a culture of accountability and responsibility among employees. The clear display of information regarding workflow progress, inventory levels, and maintenance schedules fosters transparency and encourages proactive engagement from team members. Besides, visual controls can be integrated with digital solutions to further enhance workflow management. For instance, digital displays and dashboards complemented by visual cues allow for real-time monitoring of key performance indicators and task statuses, enabling prompt decision-making and resource allocation. In an era of increasing digitalization, visual controls remain essential as they bridge the gap between manual and automated processes, ensuring seamless transitions and adaptability to changing technology. In conclusion, the effective utilization of visual controls is integral to optimizing workflow, promoting safety, and aligning with organizational standards. By incorporating visually-driven strategies into the work environment, companies can achieve significant improvements in productivity, quality, and employee satisfaction.

Implementing Digital Solutions for Order

In today's rapidly evolving business landscape, the integration of digital solutions has become a pivotal factor in enhancing operational efficiency and maintaining a competitive edge. When it comes to the 'Set in Order' phase of the 5S methodology, the implementation of digital solutions plays a crucial role in streamlining organizational processes and optimizing workspace productivity. One of the key aspects of leveraging digital tools is the transition from traditional paper-based systems to digital platforms for managing inventory, workflows, scheduling, and communication within the workplace.

Digital inventory management systems provide real-time visibility into stock levels, aiding in identifying inventory requirements, minimizing excess stock, and eliminating stockouts. These systems also facilitate the categorization and labeling of items, contributing to the systematic organization of the workspace. Moreover, digital platforms enable seamless tracking of tool and equipment locations, reducing time spent searching for resources and ensuring that items are returned to their designated places after use.

Furthermore, the incorporation of digital workflow management tools helps in standardizing processes, automating repetitive tasks, and facilitating clear communication among team members. By creating digital layouts and floor plans, organizations can visualize and optimize workspace configurations, ensuring that each item and workstation is positioned for maximum efficiency and ergonomic functionality. In addition, digital signage and visual cues can be utilized to guide employees through structured work procedures and safety protocols, thereby promoting a safe and organized work environment.

The utilization of digital solutions also extends to training and skill development, with e-learning platforms and interactive modules enabling employees to access training materials at their convenience. Through digital training initiatives, staff members can enhance their knowledge of the 'Set in Order' principles, understand the importance of maintaining order in the workplace, and learn how to effectively utilize digital tools for sustained organizational improvements.

It is important to note that while implementing digital solutions, organizations must ensure data security, user accessibility, and regular system maintenance to uphold the integrity and reliability of the digital infrastructure. As technological advancements continue to expand, businesses must remain agile in adapting new digital solutions that align with their specific operational needs and contribute to their overarching goals of creating a systematic and efficient workspace.

Staff Training and Involvement

In the pursuit of creating a systematic workspace through the 'Set in Order' phase of the 5S methodology, the role of staff training and involvement is crucial. This section delves into the various facets of training and engaging employees to make the organizational system successful and sustainable.

1. Understanding the Importance of Staff Training: It is imperative to impart knowledge about the significance of a well-organized workspace to the employees. Through comprehensive training sessions, employees can grasp the benefits of systematic order and the impact it can have on productivity, efficiency, and overall work environment.

2. Equip Employees with Organizational Skills: Training should aim to provide employees with the necessary skills to maintain an organized workspace. This includes educating them on proper storage methods, efficient space utilization, and the use of visual cues for easy navigation within the workspace.

3. Creating a Culture of Ownership: Involving employees in the decision-making process regarding the organization of their workspace can instill a sense of ownership and pride. Encouraging their active participation in suggesting improvements and implementing changes can foster a culture of accountability and responsibility.

4. Communicating the Benefits: It is important to communicate the positive impact of maintaining a systematic workspace. This can be done through regular updates, showcasing success stories, and highlighting the tangible improvements resulting from the 'Set in Order' phase. By demonstrating the benefits, employees are more likely to be motivated and engaged in the process.

5. Continuous Improvement Mentality: Staff training should also focus on instilling a mindset of continuous improvement. This involves promoting a culture where employees are encouraged to identify inefficiencies, propose solutions, and actively participate in ongoing enhancements to the organizational system.

6. Role-specific Training: Tailoring training programs to specific roles and departments can ensure that the organizational system aligns with the unique requirements of different operational areas. This targeted approach helps employees understand how systematic order benefits their specific roles and responsibilities.

7. Engagement through Recognition: Recognizing and rewarding employees who actively contribute to maintaining a well-ordered workspace fosters a sense of pride and accomplishment. Acknowledging their efforts publicly can further motivate other team members to actively participate in the process.

By investing in comprehensive staff training and promoting active involvement, organizations can ensure that the 'Set in Order' phase of the 5S methodology becomes ingrained in the culture, leading to sustained organizational efficiency and a conducive work environment.

Monitoring the Systematic Order Process

As organizations strive to maintain a high level of efficiency through systematic order, it is essential to establish robust monitoring mechanisms. Monitoring the systematic order process involves continuous observation and assessment of the implemented organizational systems with the objective of ensuring that they function optimally and contribute to overall productivity. This proactive approach allows for the early identification of any deviations or inefficiencies in the established order and enables timely corrective actions.

Effective monitoring begins with defining clear performance metrics and key performance indicators (KPIs) that align with the goals of the 'Set in Order' phase. These metrics may include measures of workflow efficiency, resource utilization, inventory accuracy, and compliance with established organizational standards. By tracking these metrics on a regular basis, organizations can gain valuable insights into the effectiveness of their systematic order processes.

Another critical aspect of monitoring involves engaging employees at all levels to participate in the observation and reporting of any issues related to systematic order. This collaborative approach promotes a culture of continuous improvement and empowers staff to take ownership of the organization's orderliness. Regular feedback from employees serves as an invaluable source of information for identifying potential areas for improvement and addressing any operational challenges that may arise.

Technology plays a significant role in modern monitoring practices, offering advanced tools for data collection, analysis, and visualization. Utilizing digital solutions such as automated monitoring systems, RFID technology, and real-time tracking software provides organizations with actionable insights into the status of their systematic order processes. These technological advancements enable swift identification of bottlenecks, irregularities, or deviations from established order standards, allowing for prompt interventions to maintain systematic order.

Continuous improvement s at the heart of monitoring the systematic order process. Organizations must be agile and adaptive in responding to changing business needs and evolving industry standards. Regular reviews and assessments of the established organizational systems are imperative to keep pace with dynamic operational requirements. This iterative approach allows for the identification of opportunities for refinement and ensures that the systematic order processes remain aligned with the overarching objectives of operational efficiency.

In conclusion, monitoring the systematic order process is paramount to sustaining the gains achieved through the 'Set in Order' phase. It involves the systematic collection of performance data, active employee engagement, leveraging technological advancements, and embracing a culture of continuous improvement. With a well-defined monitoring framework in place, organizations can proactively uphold the principles of systematic order and realize enduring benefits in productivity and operational efficiency.

Evaluating and Adjusting Organizational Systems

The process of evaluating and adjusting organizational systems is critical for ensuring the sustained effectiveness of the 'Set in Order' phase in the 5S methodology. This phase involves a thorough assessment of the implemented systematic workspace to identify areas for improvement and make necessary adjustments to enhance overall efficiency. To effectively evaluate the organizational systems, it is crucial to establish clear criteria and performance indicators that align with the goals and objectives set during the initial planning stages. These criteria may include metrics related to workflow optimization, resource utilization, waste reduction, and overall productivity. By defining specific benchmarks, organizations can accurately measure the performance of their organizational systems and identify deviations from the desired standards.

The evaluation process should involve input from personnel at various levels within the organization, including frontline employees, supervisors, and management. This inclusive approach allows for a comprehensive understanding of how the organizational systems are functioning in practice and provides valuable insights into the day-to-day challenges and opportunities for improvement. Through surveys, feedback sessions, and observational assessments, organizations can gather qualitative data on the effectiveness of the current organizational systems, as well as identify potential bottlenecks or areas of non-compliance with established standards.

In addition to qualitative assessments, quantitative measures such as time-motion studies, inventory turnover rates, and error frequency analysis can offer valuable insights into the performance of the systematic workspace. These quantitative analyses provide organizations with concrete data points to support their evaluation efforts and facilitate data-driven decision-making when considering adjustments to the organizational systems. By integrating both qualitative and quantitative approaches, organizations can gain a comprehensive understanding of the strengths and weaknesses of their current organizational systems.

Following the evaluation phase, the process of adjusting organizational systems involves implementing targeted improvements based on the findings from the evaluation. This may entail revisiting the layout of workstations, refining storage solutions, updating labeling and signage, or introducing new digital tools to enhance order and organization. It is essential for organizations to approach these adjustments with a mindset of continuous improvement, leveraging the insights gained from the evaluation process to drive meaningful enhancements. Moreover, involving employees in the adjustment phase fosters a culture of ownership and continuous improvement, empowering them to contribute to the refinement of the systematic workspace.

By iteratively evaluating and adjusting organizational systems, organizations can foster an environment of ongoing improvement and refinement, continuously striving to optimize their operational efficiency and create a workplace that supports sustained order and organization.

The First Step To A Successful Operation

Implementing 'Shine': Cleanliness as a Key to Efficiency

Introduction to 'Shine': The Principle of Workplace Cleanliness

The principle of 'Shine' represents a critical aspect of the renowned 5S methodology, focusing on the pivotal role of workplace cleanliness in fostering operational excellence. Within this context, 'Shine' underscores the broader commitment to maintaining a pristine and well-organized work environment that goes beyond mere tidiness. It encapsulates the philosophy that a clean workspace is not just a superficial attribute but is intrinsically linked to the efficiency and safety of daily operations. Embracing the concept of 'Shine' involves recognizing that the state of one's surroundings significantly influences the overall productivity and quality of work. As such, it serves as a foundational pillar in ensuring that employees have the conducive environment necessary to perform their roles effectively. By addressing cleanliness as a core tenet, organizations signal their dedication to providing an infrastructure that supports optimal working conditions. Moreover, the essence of 'Shine' extends to the promotion of safety within the workplace. A clutter-free and well-maintained setting minimizes the risk of accidents and hazards, thereby safeguarding the well-being of employees and preserving the continuity of business activities without disruptions due to preventable incidents. Consequently, the integration of 'Shine' into the organizational culture imparts a sense of responsibility among all stakeholders to prioritize cleanliness as an indispensable component of their operational conduct. This mindset shift elevates the standards for cleanliness and engenders a collective commitment to upholding these standards for mutual benefit. In summary, the introductory exploration of 'Shine' underscores its significance as a primary driver of improved workplace efficiency and safety within the overarching framework of 5S methodology.

The Benefits of a Clean Work Environment: Efficiency and Safety

Maintaining a clean work environment yields multifaceted advantages that go beyond mere aesthetics. An orderly and pristine workplace plays a pivotal role in enhancing operational efficiency and ensuring the safety of personnel. Efficiency is fostered as clutter-free spaces minimize time wastage in searching for tools and materials, enabling smoother workflows and heightened productivity. Additionally, a clean environment reduces the risk of workplace accidents and injuries, as hazards like tripping over misplaced items or encountering obscured pathways are mitigated. This translates to tangible benefits such as decreased downtime due to accidents and a notable reduction in workers' compensation claims. Furthermore, a tidy work setting reflects an organization's commitment to quality and professionalism, influencing employee morale and customer perception positively. The correlation between cleanliness and operational effectiveness underscores the indispensable value of maintaining a spotless work environment. By aligning cleanliness with improved efficiency and heightened safety, organizations can reap substantial dividends in terms of both productivity and personnel well-being.

Identifying Cleaning Needs: Tools, Equipment, and Areas

In order to effectively implement the 'Shine' principle and maintain a clean work environment, it is essential to comprehensively identify the cleaning needs within the organization. This involves a systematic assessment of the tools, equipment, and specific areas that require attention. Firstly, a thorough inventory of cleaning tools and equipment should be conducted to ensure that the right resources are available for the task at hand. This includes but is not limited to brooms, mops, vacuum cleaners, cleaning solutions, and personal protective equipment such as gloves and masks. It is imperative to verify that these items are in good working condition and readily accessible to employees. Furthermore, establishing a protocol for the regular inspection and maintenance of these tools is crucial to sustaining a high standard of cleanliness. Secondly, attention must be given to the identification of different areas within the workplace that necessitate specific cleaning requirements. This could range from common areas such as corridors, break rooms, and restrooms to more specialized zones like production floors, laboratories, and storage facilities. Each area warrants a tailored cleaning approach based on factors such as foot traffic, equipment usage, and potential hazards. By categorizing these areas and delineating their respective cleaning needs, organizations can streamline the cleaning process and ensure that all spaces receive the appropriate level of care. Finally, consideration should also be given to environmental factors that may impact cleaning needs, such as temperature, humidity, and the presence of sensitive materials. Understanding these nuances is imperative in determining optimal cleaning methods and selecting suitable cleaning products. By meticulously identifying the diverse cleaning needs pertaining to tools, equipment, and distinct areas within the workplace, organizations can lay a solid foundation for implementing the 'Shine' principle with precision and efficacy.

Establishing a Routine: Scheduling and Responsibilities

Effective implementation of the 'Shine' principle within the 5S methodology requires a meticulously planned routine that encompasses scheduling and allocation of responsibilities. By establishing a regular cleaning schedule, organizations can ensure that cleanliness becomes an integral part of their operational culture. This section focuses on the critical aspects of devising a routine, defining responsibilities, and ensuring adherence to the established cleaning practices.

Designing a comprehensive schedule involves evaluating various factors such as the size and layout of the workspace, the nature of operations conducted, and the specific cleaning requirements unique to each area. The schedule must cater to different shifts and work patterns, ensuring that every part of the facility receives the attention it demands. Moreover, the frequency of cleaning tasks should be determined based on the nature of the workspace, the potential for dirt accumulation, and the regulatory standards governing hygiene and safety.

A key aspect of establishing a successful routine is assigning clear responsibilities to individuals or teams. Each employee should understand their role in maintaining the cleanliness of the workplace. This fosters a sense of accountability and promotes collective ownership of the environment. By delineating specific tasks and areas of responsibility, any ambiguity is eliminated, and employees can perform their duties with precision and commitment.

Furthermore, setting standards for cleaning procedures is essential to ensure consistency and effectiveness. Establishing guidelines for techniques, products, and quality metrics empowers employees to carry out their assigned tasks with a clear understanding of the expected outcomes. Training on best practices and providing access to appropriate cleaning tools are crucial elements in this process, contributing to the overall success of the 'Shine' principle within the organization.

Regular review and reinforcement of the cleaning routine are imperative. Supervisors and management must monitor compliance with the schedule, provide feedback on performance, and address any emerging challenges promptly. Continuous improvement and adaptation of the cleaning routine based on feedback and evolving needs will help sustain high standards of cleanliness and efficiency throughout the workspace.

In conclusion, establishing a routine for scheduling and responsibilities is fundamental to embedding cleanliness as a core component of the organizational culture. By systematically planning and overseeing cleaning activities, organizations can create an environment that reflects professionalism, instills pride in employees, and supports the overarching goals of operational efficiency and safety.

Tools and Techniques for Effective Cleaning Procedures

To ensure the highest standards of cleanliness in the workplace, employing the right tools and techniques is paramount. Effective cleaning procedures not only contribute to a visually appealing environment but also play a crucial role in maintaining operational efficiency and ensuring the safety of employees. When selecting cleaning tools, it's important to consider the specific needs of different areas within the workspace. For instance, in manufacturing facilities, industrial vacuum cleaners equipped with HEPA filters may be necessary to effectively remove hazardous dust particles. Similarly, in office settings, microfiber cloths and eco-friendly cleaning solutions would be more suitable. Understanding the unique requirements of each area enables the implementation of tailored cleaning strategies. Techniques such as color-coding cleaning equipment can prevent cross-contamination between different work zones, thereby enhancing overall cleanliness. Additionally, employing standardized cleaning procedures, including thorough dusting, mopping, and disinfection, contributes to maintaining a pristine working environment. It's essential to provide comprehensive training to staff on the correct usage of cleaning tools and adherence to standardized procedures. This not only ensures consistent cleanliness throughout the facility but also promotes a sense of responsibility and ownership among employees. Implementing innovative technologies, such as automated floor scrubbers and UV sanitation systems, can significantly enhance the efficiency and effectiveness of cleaning processes. These advanced tools not only streamline cleaning operations but also contribute to sustainability efforts by minimizing water and chemical usage. Furthermore, establishing clear guidelines and checklists for routine inspections and maintenance of cleaning equipment is pivotal for sustained effectiveness. Regular audits can help identify areas for improvement and ensure that the cleaning tools are functioning optimally. Investing in high-quality, durable cleaning tools may require initial capital outlay, but the long-term benefits in terms of improved cleanliness, employee well-being, and productivity far outweigh the costs. Ultimately, by integrating appropriate tools and techniques into the cleaning procedures, organizations can uphold the 'Shine' principle and cultivate a workplace environment that reflects professionalism, care, and commitment to excellence.

Employee Involvement: Creating a Culture of Ownership and Pride

The successful implementation of the 'Shine' principle within an organization depends greatly on the active involvement and commitment of its employees. By fostering a culture of ownership and pride in maintaining cleanliness, companies can significantly enhance the effectiveness of their 5S initiatives. Employee involvement goes beyond mere compliance with cleaning procedures; it entails instilling a sense of responsibility and accountability for the overall cleanliness and organization of the workspace.

To achieve this, it is essential for management to communicate the importance of 'Shine' and its impact on operational efficiency and safety. Clear, transparent communication regarding expectations and the role each employee plays in maintaining cleanliness is crucial. Moreover, training programs and workshops can be conducted to educate employees on the specific cleaning standards and methods, empowering them to take ownership of the process.

Recognizing and celebrating employee contributions to maintaining a clean and organized workplace is equally vital Acknowledging and rewarding individuals or teams for their diligence and commitment to cleanliness not only reinforces positive behavior but also promotes a culture of pride and accountability. This recognition can take various forms, such as 'Cleanest Workstation' awards, public appreciation during team meetings, or inclusion in organizational newsletters or communications.

Furthermore, creating opportunities for open dialogue and feedback channels can encourage continuous improvement in cleanliness practices. Employees should feel empowered to voice their suggestions, concerns, and challenges related to maintaining cleanliness without fear of reprisal. Management should proactively seek and act on employee feedback, demonstrating that the organization values their input and actively supports their efforts to uphold cleanliness standards.

Engaging employees in the decision-making process regarding cleaning schedules, resource allocations, and improvement initiatives can further solidify their commitment to maintaining a clean work environment. By involving them in these discussions, employees feel a sense of ownership and are more likely to adhere to established cleaning protocols. Additionally, providing access to the necessary cleaning tools and supplies, along with the authority to initiate corrective actions when cleanliness standards are not met, empowers employees to actively contribute to a culture of cleanliness.

Ultimately, fostering a culture of ownership and pride in maintaining cleanliness engenders a positive work environment and contributes to overall operational excellence. When employees take pride in the cleanliness of their workspace and feel a sense of ownership over its maintenance, the 'Shine' principle becomes ingrained in the organizational culture, leading to sustained improvements in productivity, safety, and employee morale.

Monitoring and Evaluating the 'Shine' Process: Metrics and Feedback

Maintaining a consistently clean and organized work environment is crucial for the success of any organization. Once the processes for cleaning and organization are established, it is essential to monitor and evaluate the effectiveness of these efforts. This involves collecting relevant metrics and feedback to assess the impact of the 'Shine' process on efficiency and safety.

Metrics play a vital role in understanding the tangible benefits of maintaining cleanliness in the workplace. These may include observations on the reduction in waste, improved equipment reliability, decreased downtime, and enhanced employee morale. By tracking these metrics, organizations can quantify the positive outcomes of their 'Shine' initiatives and identify areas for further improvement.

In addition to quantitative measures, gathering qualitative feedback from employees is equally important. Employees are at the forefront of the workspace and can provide valuable insights into the effectiveness of the 'Shine' process. Their feedback can shed light on any potential challenges or barriers to maintaining cleanliness, as well as highlight successes and areas of improvement. Creating avenues for open communication and feedback channels fosters a culture of continuous improvement and empowers employees to take ownership of their work environment.

Utilizing technology can streamline the monitoring and evaluation process. Digital tools such as mobile applications or software platforms can be leveraged to capture real-time data on cleanliness metrics, maintenance activities, and employee feedback. These technological solutions enable efficient data collection, analysis, and reporting, providing decision-makers with actionable insights to drive improvements in the 'Shine' process.

Regular audits and assessments should be conducted to ensure compliance with cleanliness standards and to identify any deviations that require immediate attention. Establishing a structured audit schedule and involving cross-functional teams in the evaluation process promotes accountability and reinforces the importance of maintaining a clean and safe workplace. Audits also serve as opportunities to recognize and celebrate areas of excellence and to address any gaps through targeted interventions.

Ultimately, the monitoring and evaluation of the 'Shine' process are instrumental in sustaining the gains achieved through cleanliness initiatives. By consistently gathering and analyzing both quantitative metrics and qualitative feedback, organizations can adapt and enhance their cleaning practices, fostering a culture of continuous improvement and setting the foundation for operational excellence.

Addressing Common Challenges in Maintaining Cleanliness

Maintaining cleanliness within the workplace is essential for promoting a safe, productive, and efficient environment. However, numerous challenges can arise when attempting to uphold high standards of cleanliness. One common challenge involves the allocation of sufficient time and resources for cleaning activities amidst the demands of daily operations. Often, employees may feel overwhelmed by their primary responsibilities and view cleaning as an additional burden, leading to neglected areas and unsatisfactory hygiene levels.

Another prevalent obstacle pertains to sustaining employee motivation and commitment towards cleanliness. Over time, enthusiasm for maintaining a clean workspace may wane, resulting in lapses in adherence to established standards. This may be exacerbated by a lack of understanding regarding the direct impact of cleanliness on overall operational efficiency and safety.

Additionally, the complexity of modern work environments presents a unique set of challenges in cleanliness maintenance. Large-scale production facilities, for example, may have intricate machinery and equipment that are challenging to clean thoroughly. Moreover, delicate electronic components and sensitive instruments require specialized cleaning processes to prevent damage while ensuring optimal functionality.

In some cases, organizational culture and leadership approaches also present barriers to achieving and maintaining high levels of cleanliness. If management fails to emphasize the importance of cleanliness or does not provide sufficient support and resources, employees may not prioritize this aspect of their duties. Furthermore, inconsistent enforcement of cleanliness protocols can lead to confusion and disarray, undermining efforts to uphold cleanliness standards.

To effectively address these challenges, proactive measures must be implemented. This includes educating and training employees on the value of maintaining cleanliness and integrating it into daily routines. Providing adequate resources, such as quality cleaning supplies and equipment, demonstrates a commitment to upholding cleanliness standards. Encouraging teamwork and collaboration through transparent communication and recognition of efforts can foster a culture where cleanliness is collectively upheld as a shared responsibility.

Implementing regular audits and inspections enables ongoing evaluation of cleanliness standards, allowing for timely corrective measures and continuous improvement. Utilizing technology, such as automated cleaning systems and digital monitoring tools, can streamline cleaning processes, enhance precision, and reduce the burden on employees, thereby overcoming many of the aforementioned challenges. By systematically addressing these common hurdles, organizations can cultivate and sustain a workplace environment that prioritizes cleanliness as a fundamental element of operational excellence.

The Role of Technology in Enhancing 'Shine' Efforts

Technological advancements have revolutionized the way organizations approach cleanliness and maintenance within their facilities. In the context of implementing the 'Shine' principle, technology plays a pivotal role in enhancing efficiency, effectiveness, and sustainability. This section delves into the multifaceted ways in which technology can be leveraged to elevate 'Shine' efforts within a workplace environment.

One of the key areas where technology contributes to enhancing 'Shine' efforts is through the utilization of advanced cleaning equipment and machinery. Innovations such as autonomous floor scrubbers, industrial vacuums with enhanced filtration systems, and smart cleaning robots have significantly streamlined the cleaning process, making it more thorough and less time-consuming. These technologies not only improve the overall cleanliness of the workspace but also alleviate the physical burden on cleaning staff, allowing them to focus on more detail-oriented tasks.

Furthermore, the integration of sensor-based monitoring systems and Internet of Things (IoT) devices enables real-time tracking of cleanliness metrics. Smart sensors embedded in various areas of the facility can collect data on factors such as air quality, dust accumulation, and surface sanitation levels. This data, when analyzed using advanced analytics tools, provides valuable insights into patterns and trends, empowering organizations to proactively address cleanliness issues and make data-driven decisions for continuous improvement.

Another notable technological advancement that enhances 'Shine' efforts is the development of eco-friendly cleaning solutions and chemical management systems. With a growing emphasis on sustainability and environmental responsibility, organizations are turning to biodegradable cleaning agents, water-saving technologies, and energy-efficient cleaning appliances. These innovations not only contribute to a healthier and greener working environment but also align with corporate sustainability initiatives, showcasing a commitment to social and environmental stewardship.

In addition to operational enhancements, technology also facilitates training and education related to effective cleaning practices. Virtual reality (VR) simulations and interactive e-learning modules offer immersive training experiences, allowing employees to familiarize themselves with proper cleaning procedures and safety protocols in a dynamic digital environment. This immersive approach not only improves retention of information but also cultivates a culture of continuous learning and skill development among the workforce.

As organizations continue to embrace the digital transformation of their operations, the integration of technology into 'Shine' efforts becomes increasingly vital. By harnessing the power of advanced cleaning equipment, IoT-driven monitoring systems, eco-conscious solutions, and innovative training methods, businesses can elevate their commitment to cleanliness, paving the way for enhanced productivity, employee well-being, and operational excellence.

Summary and Transition to 'Standardize': Embedding Cleanliness into Daily Operations

As we conclude our exploration of 'Shine' and its critical role in workplace efficiency, it is evident that the pursuit of cleanliness is fundamental to an organization's success. The meticulous maintenance of a clean and organized workspace not only contributes to heightened productivity but also engenders a culture of respect for the work environment and a commitment to excellence. In summarizing the significance of 'Shine', it is crucial to appreciate the intertwined relationship between cleanliness and standardization. While 'Shine' emphasizes the ongoing effort to keep the workplace spotless, 'Standardize' endeavors to institutionalize these cleanliness practices as part of daily operations. The transition to 'Standardize' marks the progression from individualized cleaning efforts to the establishment of unified standards that define how cleanliness is maintained across the entire organization. This phase aims to integrate cleanliness protocols seamlessly into the fabric of operational processes, ensuring that every aspect of the working environment adheres to set standards of hygiene and order. It involves the creation and implementation of documented procedures, checklists, and visual cues that facilitate the consistent application of cleaning practices. Furthermore, 'Standardize' necessitates the alignment of duties and responsibilities among employees in upholding these standards, thereby fostering a shared commitment to maintaining a pristine workplace. The successful transition to 'Standardize' not only solidifies the gains achieved through 'Shine' but also sets the stage for the sustained enhancement of operational efficiency. By embedding cleanliness into daily operations, organizations cultivate an environment where tidiness becomes second nature and supports the seamless flow of activities. Moreover, standardized cleaning practices contribute to the overall safety and well-being of employees, as potential hazards are promptly identified and mitigated. As we embark on this transition, it is imperative to recognize that the journey towards standardization is an evolutionary process that demands patience, persistence, and continuous improvement. Embracing this phase requires an unwavering commitment from all levels of the organization, as well as a keen focus on empowering employees with the knowledge and resources essential for the successful integration of standardized cleaning processes. Consequently, the transition to 'Standardize' represents a pivotal juncture in the 5S methodology, marking the collective shift from ad-hoc cleanliness efforts to a structured framework that ingrains cleanliness as a norm within the organizational culture.

The First Step To A Successful Operation

Developing Standards: The Role of 'Standardize'

Introduction to Standardization

Standardization is a fundamental principle in the ongoing quest for organizational improvement and operational excellence. In the context of the 5S methodology, standardization plays a pivotal role in maintaining the gains achieved through the preceding stages of Sort, Set in Order, and Shine, and in ensuring sustainable efficiency. At its core, standardization involves the establishment and consistent application of set procedures, processes, and best practices across the organization. This systematic approach aims to eliminate variations, minimize waste, enhance quality, and streamline operations. By implementing standardized work practices, organizations can attain greater predictability, reliability, and overall performance consistency. The concept of standardization goes beyond mere compliance; it represents a strategic shift towards fostering a culture of continuous improvement and innovation. Standardization serves as a cornerstone for driving organizational agility and adaptability in response to dynamic market demands and technological advancements. Embracing standardization fosters a shared understanding of expectations and benchmarks within the workforce, aligning efforts towards common goals and collaborative problem-solving. Furthermore, standardization provides a framework for leveraging data-driven insights and feedback mechanisms to fine-tune processes and drive enhanced productivity. As organizations navigate increasingly complex competitive landscapes, standardization emerges as a critical enabler for achieving a harmonized and synchronized operational environment. In essence, introducing the concept of standardization within the 5S framework signifies a commitment to embedding consistency, reliability, and operational discipline into the fabric of an organization's daily operations. In the subsequent sections, we will delve deeper into the nuances of 'Standardize' within the 5S methodology, exploring practical strategies and tactics for effectively implementing and sustaining standardization to drive holistic business transformation and enduring success.

Defining 'Standardize' in the Context of 5S

The concept of 'Standardize' within the 5S methodology is a crucial pillar that contributes to operational excellence and sustained improvements. Standardization goes beyond mere uniformity; it represents the establishment of best practices, guidelines, and protocols to ensure consistency, reliability, and efficiency across all processes and operations. In the context of 5S, 'Standardize' focuses on setting clear and standardized procedures for organizing workspaces, maintaining cleanliness, and optimizing workflows.

Effective standardization involves creating a framework that minimizes variations in processes, equipment, layouts, and documentation. By doing so, organizations can eliminate waste, reduce errors, and enhance overall productivity. It also plays a pivotal role in promoting safety, as standardized procedures help mitigate potential hazards and create a secure working environment.

One fundamental aspect of 'Standardize' in the context of 5S is the development of visual management systems. These systems utilize visual cues such as color coding, labels, and signage to communicate standards, instructions, and status at a glance. They serve as powerful tools for reinforcing standardized practices, preventing deviations, and enabling swift identification of abnormalities or anomalies.

Another key element of 'Standardize' is the implementation of standardized cleaning and inspection schedules. By establishing consistent routines for maintenance and inspection, organizations can uphold cleanliness, identify potential issues early on, and ensure that equipment and facilities are in optimal condition. This proactive approach not only supports the 'Shine' principle of 5S but also contributes to the longevity of assets and machinery.

Moreover, 'Standardize' encompasses the standardization of work-in-progress inventory levels, material flow, and storage systems. By defining optimal inventory levels and streamlining material handling processes, organizations can minimize excess inventory, reduce lead times, and facilitate smoother production flows. This leads to improved resource utilization and enables better responsiveness to changes in demand.

Further, in the context of 5S, 'Standardize' extends to the standardization of work instructions, quality control measures, and performance metrics. Clear, standardized documentation, along with defined quality parameters, aids in ensuring that tasks are executed consistently and outputs meet predetermined quality standards. Concurrently, standardized performance metrics provide a basis for evaluating adherence to standards and identifying opportunities for refinement.

In summary, 'Standardize' serves as the cornerstone for fostering stability, predictability, and orderliness within an organization. Embracing standardization not only drives continuous improvement but also cultivates a culture of discipline, precision, and accountability. As organizations delve deeper into the realm of 'Standardize,' they pave the way for sustainable growth and operational excellence, laying the groundwork for the next phase of the 5S journey: 'Sustain.'

Core Principles of Effective Standardization

The effective standardization of processes within the 5S methodology is crucial to achieving and sustaining operational efficiency. This section will delve into the core principles that underpin successful standardization efforts. Firstly, it's essential to understand that standardization doesn't mean rigidity; rather, it aims to provide a framework for consistency and improvement. One key principle is the alignment of standardization with the overall organizational goals and objectives. By ensuring that standardization efforts are directly linked to the strategic vision of the organization, it becomes easier to garner support and participation from all levels of the workforce. Moreover, clear communication of standardized processes, along with the rationale behind them, is vital. Employees are more likely to embrace and adhere to standards when they understand the benefits and the reasoning behind them. Another fundamental principle is the involvement of frontline employees in the development and refinement of standards. This not only enhances the quality of standards but also fosters a sense of ownership and accountability among the workforce. A structured approach to standardization, which includes documenting procedures and best practices, is integral to ensure that everyone is working from the same playbook. Additionally, embedding a culture of continuous improvement within the standardization process is pivotal. This means that standards should not be viewed as static; instead, there should be mechanisms in place to regularly review and update them based on feedback and changing requirements. Furthermore, the standardization process should be designed to promote flexibility where necessary, allowing for adaptation to specific circumstances without compromising overall consistency. Lastly, metrics and key performance indicators (KPIs) tied to standardized processes should be established to monitor adherence and measure the impact of standardization on operational performance. These core principles form the bedrock of effective standardization within the 5S framework, paving the way for sustained improvements in efficiency and quality.

Establishing Reference Points and Benchmarks

In the pursuit of standardization within the 5S framework, it is imperative to establish clear reference points and benchmarks that serve as the foundation for evaluating and maintaining consistent performance levels. Reference points act as the starting line, providing a tangible measure from which progress can be gauged while benchmarks define the desired standards to be achieved. This section will delve into the significance of establishing these essential elements and the methods through which they can be effectively implemented.

A key aspect in establishing reference points and benchmarks is the alignment with organizational goals and industry standards. By identifying specific targets that are in harmony with broader objectives, businesses can ensure that their standardization efforts are directly contributing to overall success. These targets should encapsulate not only efficiency and productivity metrics, but also quality, safety, and compliance criteria relevant to the organization's operational context.

Furthermore, the process of setting reference points and benchmarks necessitates a comprehensive analysis of current practices and performance levels. This involves gathering data on existing workflows, output levels, and qualitative aspects relevant to the 5S methodology. Additionally, market research and best practice comparisons can offer valuable insights into industry standards and serve as references for setting internal benchmarks.

Once the reference points and benchmarks have been identified, the next step involves translating these into actionable, measurable targets. This might entail creating visual aids such as process maps and performance dashboards to communicate the standardization goals across the organization. Clear communication and transparency regarding these targets are paramount to ensuring alignment and commitment throughout the workforce.

Another crucial consideration in establishing reference points and benchmarks is the need for continual review and adjustment. As operational dynamics evolve, so too must the reference points and benchmarks be re-evaluated to ensure they remain pertinent and reflective of current best practices. In essence, this ensures that the 5S standards stay adaptable and responsive to changing business environments and requirements.

In summary, the establishment of reference points and benchmarks represents a fundamental pillar in the quest for effective standardization within the 5S methodology. By aligning with organizational objectives, rigorously analyzing current practices, and fostering continual review, businesses can lay the groundwork for sustained improvement and operational excellence.

Tools and Techniques for Standardization

Standardization serves as the backbone of operational efficiency, ensuring consistency, quality, and reliability in processes across an organization. To effectively implement and maintain standardized practices, it is crucial to employ a wide array of tools and techniques that support the standardization process.

A critical tool for standardization is the development of detailed work instructions and procedures. These documents provide clear guidance on how tasks should be performed, outlining the necessary steps, parameters, and best practices. By creating comprehensive work instructions, organizations can minimize variation in processes and enhance overall quality and consistency.

Another essential technique for standardization is the use of visual management tools such as color-coded labels, signage, and shadow boards. Visual cues serve as a universal language, enabling employees to quickly identify tools, materials, and work areas. Additionally, visual management aids in sustaining standardized practices by making deviations from the standard immediately apparent, prompting corrective action.

Furthermore, the implementation of standard operating procedures (SOPs) supported by digital platforms and software solutions can significantly streamline and enforce standardized processes. These systems allow for the efficient documentation, dissemination, and revision of procedures, ensuring that all team members have access to the most current standards and guidelines at their fingertips.

In continuous improvement initiatives, the use of lean management tools such as value stream mapping, Gemba walks, and root cause analysis are invaluable for identifying opportunities for standardization. These tools enable organizations to gain deep insights into their processes, pinpoint inefficiencies, and systematically develop standardized solutions that optimize workflow and eliminate waste.

Moreover, statistical process control (SPC) techniques play a pivotal role in standardization by providing a structured approach to monitoring and controlling key process variables. Through the application of statistical methods and control charts, organizations can ensure that their processes operate within established tolerances, maintaining consistency and predictability.

Lastly, fostering a culture of empowerment and accountability among employees through training, coaching, and recognition programs is essential for successful standardization. By equipping team members with the knowledge and skills to uphold standards, and recognizing their contributions to maintaining standards, organizations can cultivate a workforce that embraces and takes ownership of standardized processes.

When implemented collectively, these tools and techniques form a robust framework for standardization, driving sustainable improvements in quality, efficiency, and operational excellence within an organization.

Role of Leadership in Enforcing Standards

In the realm of operational excellence and organizational effectiveness, the role of leadership in enforcing standards cannot be overstated. Leaders serve as the driving force behind the successful implementation and sustenance of standardized practices within the workplace. They play a crucial role in setting the tone, expectations, and accountability for adhering to the established standards. The influence of leadership extends across all levels of the organization, from frontline employees to middle management and executive leadership. One of the primary responsibilities of leaders is to communicate the importance of standards clearly and consistently. This involves articulating the rationale behind the standards, their alignment with organizational goals, and the benefits they bring to the overall operational efficiency. Moreover, leaders must lead by example, demonstrating their own commitment to adhering to the standards and participating actively in the standardization processes. Their visible participation fosters a culture of accountability and dedication to quality and consistency at every level. Another critical aspect of leadership's role in standard enforcement is the establishment of a supportive infrastructure. This entails providing the necessary resources, training, and support systems to enable employees to meet the set standards effectively. It also involves creating channels for feedback and continuous improvement, ensuring that the standards remain relevant and practical in the evolving work environment. Furthermore, leaders must prioritize recognition and reinforcement of adherence to standards. By acknowledging and rewarding individuals and teams who consistently meet or exceed the standards, leaders reinforce the value of compliance while inspiring others to strive for excellence. Communication is instrumental in leadership's efforts to enforce standards. Clear, frequent communication regarding performance expectations, updates on standards, and feedback on adherence is essential for building understanding and fostering a sense of ownership among employees. Finally, effective leadership encompasses monitoring and accountability. Leaders are responsible for regularly evaluating the implementation of standards, identifying areas for improvement, and addressing any deviations from the set norms promptly and constructively. Such oversight ensures that the standards are not only established but also effectively enforced and continuously refined to reflect the changing needs of the organization and industry. In summary, the role of leadership in enforcing standards is pivotal to the success of any standardization initiative. Their commitment, communication, support, and oversight are indispensable elements in embedding a culture of continuous improvement and excellence within the organization.

Training and Development: Building Competence

In the pursuit of operational excellence through 5S methodology, the aspect of 'Training and Development' assumes paramount significance. Building competence within the workforce is not merely a box-ticking exercise, but a strategic investment in the organization's long-term success. Effective training programs are pivotal in facilitating employee engagement, standard adherence, and overall process improvement. This section delves into the core strategies and best practices for cultivating competence through targeted training and development initiatives.

A holistic approach to training begins with a comprehensive analysis of the existing skill gaps and proficiency levels across different roles and functions within the organizational framework. Identifying these gaps paves the way for the design and implementation of tailored training modules that cater to the unique requirements of various teams and individuals. Whether it involves on-the-job training, workshops, virtual seminars, or e-learning platforms, the delivery of content should align with the preferred learning styles and schedules of employees, fostering a culture of continuous learning.

Moreover, building competence necessitates the integration of practical hands-on experiences, allowing employees to apply newly acquired knowledge in real-world scenarios. By immersing individuals in simulations, problem-solving exercises, and cross-functional projects, organizations can instill a deeper understanding of 5S principles and their relevance to day-to-day operations. Encouraging collaboration and knowledge sharing further amplifies the impact of training, as employees broaden their perspectives and adopt a collective ownership of standardized processes.

Furthermore, a robust training and development strategy places emphasis on leadership mentoring and succession planning. Nurturing future leaders who embody the values of 5S and champion its implementation becomes a critical facet of sustaining operational excellence. Mentorship programs, career progression frameworks, and performance-based incentives play a pivotal role in nurturing a cohort of competent individuals capable of upholding established standards and driving continuous improvement initiatives.

Lastly, an ongoing evaluation and enhancement process is imperative to ensure the effectiveness of training and development efforts. Regular feedback mechanisms, post-training assessments, and performance evaluations provide crucial insights into the impact of learning interventions, enabling refinement and adaptation to evolving organizational needs. It is through this iterative process of learning, application, and refinement that organizations cultivate a truly competent workforce committed to the principles of 5S and geared towards achieving sustainable operational excellence.

Monitoring and Reviewing Established Standards

To ensure the effectiveness and relevance of established standards within the framework of 5S, it is imperative to implement a robust system for monitoring and reviewing these standards on a regular basis. Monitoring involves the continuous observation and assessment of how well the established standards are being adhered to in the workplace. This can be achieved through regular audits, checks, and visual management tools that provide real-time feedback on the state of adherence to the standards.

In addition, reviewing the established standards involves periodic assessments to evaluate their efficacy in improving operational efficiency, safety, and overall productivity. This process necessitates gathering feedback from employees at all levels, including those directly involved in the implementation and those impacted by the standards. This holistic approach ensures that the standards are not only practical but also align with the actual needs and challenges faced within the organization.

Furthermore, the review process should encompass an examination of key performance indicators (KPIs) related to the standards. These KPIs serve as quantitative measures of the impact of the standards on various aspects of operations. They provide valuable insights into areas of success as well as potential shortcomings, guiding the refinement and adjustment of standards where necessary.

A crucial aspect of monitoring and reviewing established standards is the documentation of findings and any identified deviations from the set norms. This documentation serves as a repository of historical data that can be analyzed to identify recurring issues, trends, and areas for improvement. It also provides transparency and accountability, enabling stakeholders to track the progress and evolution of the standards over time.

Equally important is the establishment of a cross-functional team responsible for overseeing the monitoring and review process. This team should comprise individuals representing different departments and functions to ensure diverse perspectives and expertise in the evaluation of standards. Their collective insights and contributions enrich the review process and promote a comprehensive understanding of the standards' impact across the organization.

Ultimately, the process of monitoring and reviewing established standards is a dynamic endeavor that requires continuous attention and adaptation. By fostering a culture of continuous improvement, organizations can leverage the insights gained from this process to refine existing standards, identify new areas for standardization, and drive ongoing enhancements in operational excellence.

Adapting Standards for Continuous Improvement

Standards within the context of the 5S methodology are not static; instead, they should constantly evolve to meet the changing needs of the organization and its processes. Adapting standards for continuous improvement is a crucial aspect of sustaining the gains achieved through the implementation of 5S. This section explores the intricacies of adapting standards to foster ongoing enhancements in operational efficiency and workplace organization.

Adapting standards begins with a mindset shift towards embracing change as a fundamental driver of improvement. Organizations must cultivate a culture that encourages feedback, innovation, and flexibility in adhering to established standards. By fostering an environment where employees are empowered to propose modifications to existing standards based on their frontline experiences, companies can harness the collective wisdom of their workforce to drive impactful changes.

To facilitate effective adaptation of standards, it is paramount to establish robust mechanisms for soliciting, evaluating, and implementing suggested improvements. Regular forums such as improvement workshops, suggestion schemes, or quality circles can serve as avenues for employees to put forth their ideas for refining standards. These should be complemented by structured review processes led by cross-functional teams, ensuring that proposed changes are thoroughly assessed for their potential impact on workflow, safety, and overall productivity.

Moreover, the adaptation of standards necessitates a diligent approach to documentation and communication. Clear channels for disseminating revised standards and procedures must be established to ensure that all relevant stakeholders are informed about the changes and trained accordingly. Leveraging digital platforms and accessible repositories for standard operating procedures (SOPs) can streamline this process, enabling seamless updates and access to the latest versions of established standards.

A critical element of adapting standards involves integrating feedback loops into the monitoring and review mechanisms. Continuously gathering data on the efficacy of updated standards and soliciting real-time feedback from employees allows for iterative refinement and optimization. Measurement metrics such as key performance indicators (KPIs) and process control parameters play a pivotal role in objectively assessing the impact of adjusted standards, guiding further iterations and adjustments as necessary.

Furthermore, adaptive standards should align with broader organizational objectives and evolving industry best practices. As market dynamics and customer expectations transform, businesses must ensure that their standards remain attuned to these shifts. This necessitates staying abreast of emerging technologies, regulatory requirements, and benchmarking against peer organizations to validate the relevance and competitiveness of the adapted standards.

In conclusion, the process of adapting standards for continuous improvement is not merely about reacting to immediate issues but embracing a proactive approach to driving sustainable progress. By institutionalizing a culture of adaptability and agility, organizations can leverage the power of dynamic standards to continually elevate their operational effectiveness and responsiveness to market demands.

Conclusion and Transition to 'Sustain'

As we conclude our exploration of the role of 'Standardize' in the 5S methodology, it becomes clear that the establishment of standards is not a one-time effort but an ongoing process deeply integrated into the organization's culture. Adapting standards for continuous improvement involves a mindset shift towards agility, where the emphasis is not just on adhering to existing standards, but also on actively seeking ways to enhance them. It is essential for organizations to recognize that standardization lays the foundation for sustained operational excellence. The attention to detail required in the standardization phase directly impacts the ability to 'Sustain' the improvements achieved through 5S.

Transitioning to 'Sustain' signifies a crucial shift in mindset from implementation to long-term maintenance. It involves embedding the 5S practices into the daily routines and ensuring that the standards set during the 'Standardize' phase are upheld consistently. Furthermore, sustaining the gains made through 5S demands disciplined adherence to the established norms and continuous vigilance against complacency. The transition to 'Sustain' implies a proactive approach to prevent regression back to previous work habits and environments.

In this phase, the organizational focus moves from creating change to cultivating a culture where the new way of working becomes the norm. Emphasizing employee engagement and empowerment plays a pivotal role in ensuring that the standards are sustained effectively. Leadership must continue to support and encourage the workforce in upholding the established standards while also facilitating the identification and resolution of any obstacles that may hinder sustainability.

Sustaining improved practices leads to the consolidation of gains and sets the stage for further advancements. The 'Sustain' phase is not merely about preserving the current state but also about fostering an environment that thrives on innovation and continual enhancement. To achieve this, organizations need to integrate mechanisms for feedback and improvement into their sustenance strategy, enabling an adaptive response to evolving challenges and opportunities.

Ultimately, successful sustainment of 5S requires a holistic approach that transcends mere compliance with standards. It demands a cultural transformation where the principles of 5S become ingrained in the fabric of the organization, driving continual improvement and responsiveness to change. The journey from 'Standardize' to 'Sustain' encapsulates the essence of 5S – a journey from establishing order and discipline to nurturing a culture of excellence and resilience.

The First Step To A Successful Operation

'Sustain': Maintaining Gains Over Time

Introduction to Sustaining 5S Practices

Examination of the foundational principles of maintaining 5S practices over time is crucial to the long-term success and sustainability of organizational efficiency efforts. Sustaining 5S practices requires a comprehensive understanding of not only the methodology's individual components but also their interconnectedness and the broader impact on the organizational culture and operations. To effectively sustain 5S practices, it is essential to ensure that all employees are equipped with the necessary knowledge and skills. This necessitates the development and implementation of comprehensive training programs that cater to diverse roles and responsibilities within the organization. Continuous education initiatives play a pivotal role in instilling a culture of ongoing improvement and adaptation, empowering employees to embrace change and take ownership of sustaining 5S practices. Beyond training, sustaining 5S practices entails fostering a supportive infrastructure within the organization. Establishing designated support teams or champions who can guide and assist in the implementation of 5S practices across different departments is critical. Additionally, providing access to resources such as visual aids, standard operating procedures, and best practice guidelines facilitates the seamless integration of 5S into daily operations. Another fundamental aspect of sustaining 5S practices entails embedding the principles into the fabric of the organizational culture. This involves promoting a mindset of continuous improvement, where every employee is encouraged to contribute ideas for enhancing processes and eliminating waste. Such cultural integration reinforces the significance of 5S and ensures that it becomes ingrained in the organization's values and behaviors. Moreover, regular audits and reviews serve as indispensable tools for monitoring and maintaining 5S practices. These assessments provide actionable insights into areas that require corrective actions or further improvement, allowing the organization to address issues proactively. They also facilitate the identification of success stories and exemplary practices that can be shared across the organization, fostering a culture of recognition and continuous learning. Lastly, sustaining 5S practices necessitates aligning performance metrics with 5S objectives and regularly monitoring key indicators. By establishing clear performance targets and regularly tracking progress, organizations can identify deviations early on and implement timely interventions to uphold the integrity of 5S practices. Furthermore, feedback mechanisms should be implemented to gather input from employees on their experiences with sustaining 5S practices, enabling continuous learning and refinement of strategies. In essence, sustaining 5S practices demands a multifaceted approach that encompasses training, support structures, cultural integration, monitoring, and continuous adaptation.

The Role of Training and Continuous Education

Training and continuous education play a pivotal role in the sustained success of 5S practices within an organization. It is through comprehensive training programs that employees at all levels not only gain an understanding of the underlying principles and objectives of 5S but also acquire the necessary skills to implement and sustain these practices effectively. By investing in training, organizations demonstrate their commitment to providing the knowledge and tools essential for employees to excel in maintaining a standardized, organized, and efficient work environment.

Continuous education ensures that employees are kept informed about any updates or modifications to the 5S methodology, as well as new technologies or best practices that can further enhance its implementation. This ongoing learning process can take various forms, including workshops, seminars, webinars, and online resources. Moreover, organizations can also encourage employees to pursue relevant certifications or accreditations, thereby fostering a culture of continuous improvement and expertise in 5S methodologies.

Effective training and continuous education also contribute to employee motivation and engagement. When individuals understand the significance of 5S in improving workplace safety, productivity, and overall organizational performance, they are more likely to actively participate in its sustainability. Engaging, interactive training sessions and educational materials can inspire a sense of ownership and pride in maintaining 5S standards, empowering employees to take responsibility for the cleanliness, orderliness, and efficiency of their work areas.

Furthermore, training and continuous education facilitate the dissemination of best practices and success stories within the organization. Through knowledge-sharing platforms and collaborative learning environments, employees can exchange experiences and insights, learning from each other's challenges and triumphs in sustaining 5S over time. This collective wisdom not only strengthens the support structure for 5S but also fosters a sense of community and shared dedication to its long-term success.

In conclusion, the role of training and continuous education in sustaining 5S practices cannot be overstated. Organizations that prioritize ongoing learning and skill development regarding 5S methodologies are better equipped to maintain the gains achieved through its implementation, fostering a culture of excellence, innovation, and operational efficiency.

Establishing a Strong Support Structure

Building a strong support structure is essential for the successful sustainability of 5S practices within an organization. This support structure should encompass various levels of the hierarchy, from frontline employees to upper management, and should be rooted in a collective commitment to maintaining a culture of efficiency and continuous improvement.

At the core of this support structure is leadership buy-in. Without visible and vocal support from organizational leaders, the efforts to sustain 5S practices may falter. Leaders must communicate the importance of 5S sustainability, allocate resources for its maintenance, and actively participate in the process. Establishing a dedicated cross-functional team responsible for overseeing 5S implementation and sustainability can further bolster the support structure. This team can serve as champions for 5S, ensuring its integration into daily operations and driving continuous improvement initiatives.

Moreover, providing adequate training and resources to employees is crucial. By empowering individuals with the necessary knowledge and tools to uphold 5S principles, the organization fosters a sense of ownership and accountability in all team members. This empowerment should be complemented by creating avenues for feedback and suggestions, encouraging a collaborative approach to sustaining 5S practices.

Another facet of a robust support structure involves establishing clear roles and responsibilities related to 5S. Each individual should understand their role in maintaining the established standards and be held accountable for their contributions to sustaining the 5S initiative. By aligning performance evaluations and recognition programs with 5S efforts, the organization reinforces the importance of these practices throughout the workforce.

Lastly, leveraging technology and digital tools can streamline the support structure and facilitate the sustainability of 5S. Implementing digital platforms for tracking progress, sharing best practices, and identifying areas for improvement can enhance the transparency and effectiveness of the support system.

In conclusion, establishing a strong support structure for 5S sustainability requires a multi-faceted approach that encompasses leadership commitment, employee empowerment, cross-functional collaboration, defined roles, and technological enablement. This robust support structure serves as the backbone that upholds the principles of 5S over time, ensuring that the gains achieved through its implementation endure and continue to drive operational excellence.

Embedding 5S into Organizational Culture

Embedding 5S principles into the organizational culture is a pivotal step towards sustaining gains over time. It involves integrating the core values of 5S - Sort, Set in Order, Shine, Standardize, and Sustain - into the fabric of the company's operations, processes, and behaviors. A successful cultural embedding of 5S fosters a mindset where maintaining a clean, organized, and efficient workspace becomes second nature.

Achieving this integration requires strong leadership commitment and consistent communication to reinforce the importance of 5S practices. Leaders must lead by example, visibly demonstrating their adherence to 5S principles and actively participating in improvement activities. By doing so, they motivate employees to embrace 5S as a standard way of working rather than a temporary initiative.

In addition to leadership buy-in, employee involvement is crucial for the cultural assimilation of 5S. Organizations should encourage and empower employees at all levels to take ownership of 5S initiatives, fostering a sense of responsibility for their work environment. This empowerment can be achieved through regular training, recognition of 5S contributions, and providing the necessary resources to maintain and improve workspace organization.

The integration of 5S into the organizational culture also involves aligning the performance management and reward systems with 5S goals. Recognizing and rewarding individuals and teams that exemplify 5S principles reinforces the desired behaviors and motivates others to follow suit. Conversely, addressing deviations from 5S standards in a constructive manner helps maintain accountability and consistency across the organization.

Moreover, fostering a culture of continuous improvement complements the sustainability of 5S by encouraging employees to seek innovative ways to enhance workplace organization and efficiency. This can be accomplished through platforms for idea generation, cross-functional collaboration, and learning from best practices within and outside the organization. Emphasizing the value of feedback and embracing a mindset of adaptability further solidifies the assimilation of 5S into the organizational culture.

Ultimately, embedding 5S into the organizational culture demands dedication, persistence, and a long-term perspective. It requires ongoing reinforcement, open communication, and a steadfast commitment to integrating 5S principles into the daily operations and mindset of every individual within the organization.

Utilizing Regular Audits and Reviews

Regular audits and reviews are essential components of sustaining the gains achieved through the implementation of the 5S methodology. These processes serve as critical checkpoints to ensure that the established standards and practices are being consistently followed and adhered to across all levels of the organization. By conducting regular audits, teams can identify any deviations from the prescribed 5S standards and address them promptly, thereby preventing potential deterioration in cleanliness, order, and overall efficiency.

The audit process should be methodical and thorough, encompassing all areas and processes within the organization. It is important to establish clear criteria and benchmarks for each aspect of 5S, allowing auditors to objectively evaluate compliance and performance. Utilizing standardized audit checklists can streamline this process, ensuring that all relevant aspects are systematically assessed and documented during the review.

Furthermore, the review phase following the audit is equally crucial. It provides an opportunity to analyze the findings, identify recurring issues, and recognize exemplary adherence to 5S principles. Reviews should not solely focus on identifying non-conformities but also celebrate successes and best practices. This balanced approach fosters a culture of continuous improvement and encourages employees to actively contribute to maintaining high 5S standards.

In addition to internal audits and reviews, organizations can benefit from periodic external assessments or benchmarking exercises. Engaging external experts or consultants can provide valuable insights and fresh perspectives, helping the organization stay abreast of industry best practices and innovative approaches to 5S sustainability.

It is advisable to integrate technology into the audit and review processes to enhance efficiency and accuracy. Digital tools and software can facilitate data collection, analysis, and visualization of audit results, enabling real-time tracking of performance trends and areas requiring attention. Leveraging such technological advancements can streamline the entire audit and review workflow, allowing for more proactive decision-making and actionable insights.

Ultimately, the effective utilization of regular audits and reviews serves as a cornerstone for continual enhancement of 5S practices, reinforcing the commitment to operational excellence and sustained improvement.

Employee Engagement and Ownership

Employee engagement and ownership are critical factors in maintaining the gains achieved through the implementation of 5S methodology. With their direct involvement and commitment, employees become crucial stakeholders in the sustainability of efficient work practices. Engaging employees in the 5S process fosters a sense of ownership and responsibility for the workspace, leading to increased productivity, morale, and overall organizational success. This section will delve into the strategies and best practices for fostering employee engagement and ownership within the framework of 5S.

One of the fundamental approaches to promoting employee engagement is through transparent communication. Providing clear information about the 5S goals, benefits, and expected contributions empowers employees to understand the significance of their roles in sustaining the 5S practices. When employees comprehend how their efforts contribute to the organization's overall success, they are more likely to take ownership of their assigned work areas and actively participate in maintaining the established standards.

In addition to communication, involving employees in the decision-making process regarding workspace organization and workflow improvements can significantly enhance their sense of ownership. By seeking their input and incorporating their ideas, employees feel valued and empowered to take an active role in shaping their work environment. This participatory approach not only leads to more effective solutions but also creates a culture of continuous improvement that aligns with the core principles of 5S.

A crucial aspect of fostering employee engagement and ownership is recognizing and rewarding their contributions towards sustaining the 5S initiatives. Acknowledging and celebrating individual and team accomplishments in maintaining a standardized, organized, and efficient workspace reinforces the desired behaviors. Recognition programs, performance incentives, and opportunities for skill development further motivate employees to embrace their responsibilities in upholding the 5S principles.

Moreover, providing adequate training and resources enables employees to fully understand the 5S methodology and equips them with the necessary skills to take ownership of their designated work areas. This includes educating them on the principles of waste reduction, visual management, and workplace organization, empowering them to identify and address inefficiencies as part of their daily tasks.

To foster sustainable employee engagement and ownership, it is essential for leadership to promote a supportive and inclusive work culture that values collaboration, open feedback, and continuous learning. Leaders should serve as role models by actively participating in 5S activities and demonstrating their commitment to maintaining high standards within the workplace. By creating an environment where employees feel respected, heard, and empowered, organizations can cultivate a workforce that embraces 5S as a way of life, ensuring long-term success and continuous improvement.

Adapting to Changes and Continuous Improvement

In today's dynamic business environment, the ability to adapt to changes and continuously improve is crucial for the sustained success of any organization. Embracing a culture of continuous improvement involves a proactive approach towards identifying and responding to shifts in market conditions, technological advancements, and customer preferences. As part of the 5S methodology, the principle of 'Sustain' necessitates not only maintaining existing standards but also fostering an environment that welcomes change and innovation.

Continuous improvement requires a mindset shift among employees at all levels within an organization. This involves encouraging a culture of open communication and idea-sharing, where every individual feels empowered to contribute towards the enhancement of processes and workflows. It also entails promoting a willingness to experiment with new approaches and methodologies to drive efficiency and effectiveness. Leadership plays a pivotal role in setting the tone for embracing change, empowering teams to explore new opportunities and methods for improvement.

The process of adapting to changes involves the systematic analysis of current practices, systems, and procedures. It requires a thorough understanding of the root causes of inefficiencies or bottlenecks and a structured approach to addressing them. Implementing feedback loops and mechanisms for soliciting input from employees across different departments can provide valuable insights into areas that require improvement. This collaborative approach not only engages employees in the process but also ensures that diverse perspectives are considered when implementing changes.

Moreover, continuous improvement is closely tied to the concept of lean management, which advocates for the elimination of waste and the optimization of resources. By continuously evaluating processes and workflows, organizations can identify areas of redundancy or unnecessary complexity and restructure them to achieve greater efficiency. This may involve adopting new technologies, redefining standard operating procedures, or reorganizing workspaces to minimize unnecessary movements and delays.

Organizations committed to continuous improvement also recognize the significance of measuring progress through relevant metrics and performance indicators. These measurements can range from productivity and quality metrics to employee satisfaction and customer feedback. By tracking key performance indicators, organizations can gain insights into the impact of changes and improvements, enabling data-driven decision-making and accountability.

In conclusion, the journey towards sustaining gains over time through the 5S methodology involves embracing a culture of continuous improvement and adaptability. By fostering a workplace environment that encourages innovation, collaboration, and data-driven decision-making, organizations can navigate changes effectively and drive long-term success.

Monitoring Metrics and Performance Indicators

Monitoring metrics and performance indicators are instrumental in evaluating the effectiveness of 5S practices over time. This section will explore the key metrics and indicators that organizations can utilize to track the impact of 5S implementation and ensure sustained improvements in operational efficiency.

One of the primary metrics for measuring the success of 5S is the overall equipment effectiveness (OEE). OEE provides a holistic view of equipment utilization, quality performance, and production efficiency. By tracking OEE before and after the implementation of 5S, organizations can quantify the tangible benefits derived from the methodology, such as reduced downtime, improved productivity, and enhanced product quality.

Another crucial performance indicator is the rate of non-conformance or defects. A lower rate of defects signifies that 5S practices have positively influenced the quality of output and reduced waste in the production process. Additionally, organizations may measure the cycle time and lead time for processes to assess the impact of 5S on workflow efficiency.

Furthermore, it's essential to monitor employee engagement and participation in sustaining the 5S principles. Surveys, feedback mechanisms, and participation rates in improvement initiatives serve as qualitative indicators of how well the workforce has embraced and internalized 5S methodologies. Regularly assessing these factors enables organizations to address any shortcomings and continuously reinforce the importance of 5S among employees.

In addition to these internal metrics, external benchmarks and industry standards can also be used to gauge the effectiveness of 5S implementation. Comparing key performance indicators with industry averages and best practices allows organizations to identify areas for further improvement and innovation.

Central to effective monitoring of metrics and performance indicators is the use of robust data collection and analysis tools. Leveraging technology solutions for real-time data capture, visualization, and reporting empowers decision-makers to make informed choices and drive continual improvement initiatives based on reliable insights.

Ultimately, the sustained success of 5S implementation depends on the diligent monitoring of various metrics and performance indicators. Organizations that prioritize this aspect of the methodology demonstrate a commitment to long-term excellence and continuous progress in operational efficiency.

Feedback Mechanisms for Continuous Learning

Feedback mechanisms play a crucial role in the continuous improvement of 5S practices. Effective feedback serves as a channel through which employees and teams can receive constructive input regarding their application of 5S principles and identify areas for enhancement. It empowers individuals to reflect on their performance, make necessary adjustments, and contribute to the collective efforts towards sustained operational excellence. In this section, we will explore various feedback mechanisms that foster continuous learning within the context of 5S implementation.

One key feedback mechanism is establishing regular performance reviews and assessments. Through periodic evaluations, both at individual and team levels, organizations can gauge the effectiveness of 5S practices and gather valuable insights into areas needing development. These reviews should be conducted in a supportive manner, providing employees with specific feedback on their adherence to 5S standards and offering actionable recommendations for improvement.

Another effective feedback mechanism involves creating open communication channels, such as suggestion boxes, digital platforms, or regular team meetings, where employees can share observations, ideas, and concerns related to 5S. Encouraging transparent dialogue fosters a culture of continuous improvement and allows for the identification of potential obstacles to sustained 5S success.

Furthermore, peer-to-peer feedback and mentorship programs can be instrumental in promoting continuous learning. By enabling employees to offer constructive feedback to their colleagues based on their own experiences and expertise, organizations foster a collaborative learning environment. Pairing seasoned employees with new hires or those unfamiliar with 5S methodologies can facilitate knowledge transfer and skill development, ultimately contributing to the sustained integration of 5S practices.

Organizations should also consider leveraging technology to facilitate feedback mechanisms. Digital surveys, mobile applications, or feedback tracking systems can provide real-time insight into the effectiveness of 5S initiatives and allow for immediate corrective actions. Additionally, incorporating automated feedback processes into daily operations, such as quick checklists or assessment tools, promotes consistent monitoring and timely adjustments.

In summary, implementing comprehensive feedback mechanisms within the framework of 5S is essential for nurturing a culture of continuous learning and improvement. By embracing diverse channels for feedback, from formal reviews to informal dialogues, organizations can instill a commitment to ongoing enhancement, thereby securing the long-term sustainability of 5S practices.

Long-term Strategic Planning and 5S Sustainability

Long-term strategic planning is vital for achieving and sustaining the benefits of the 5S methodology within an organization. While initial implementation of 5S may yield immediate improvements in efficiency and productivity, long-term sustainability requires a comprehensive strategic approach. This section will delve into the key elements of long-term strategic planning for 5S sustainability.

One of the fundamental elements of long-term strategic planning for 5S sustainability is the alignment of 5S objectives with the overall organizational goals. This involves integrating 5S principles into the organization's mission, vision, and strategic plans, ensuring that 5S becomes an integral part of the company's culture and operations. By embedding 5S into the fabric of the organization, the sustained benefits of the methodology can be realized over the long term.

Additionally, long-term strategic planning necessitates the development of a robust framework for continuous improvement, which encompasses the ongoing evolution and refinement of 5S practices. This framework should include mechanisms for identifying emerging opportunities for improvement, adapting to changes in the internal and external environment, and continuously enhancing the 5S processes to align with evolving business needs. Moreover, it should facilitate the seamless integration of 5S with other operational excellence initiatives, such as Lean and Six Sigma, to create synergies and maximize overall impact.

Furthermore, a key consideration in long-term strategic planning for 5S sustainability is the allocation of sufficient resources and support for maintaining the momentum of 5S initiatives. This includes dedicating adequate budget, personnel, and technology to uphold the 5S standards and drive continuous adherence to best practices. Effective resource management and support are essential in ensuring that 5S does not regress over time, but rather flourishes and becomes deeply ingrained in the organizational fabric.

An integral aspect of long-term strategic planning for 5S sustainability involves the establishment of a robust governance structure that oversees the ongoing execution and evolution of 5S. This entails defining clear roles and responsibilities, instituting regular performance reviews and evaluations, and fostering accountability at all levels of the organization. A well-defined governance structure provides the necessary oversight and guidance to sustain 5S practices effectively.

In conclusion, long-term strategic planning is instrumental in ensuring the enduring success of 5S initiatives within organizations. By aligning 5S with organizational goals, fostering continuous improvement, allocating adequate resources, and establishing a robust governance structure, companies can achieve sustainable 5S excellence. The meticulous attention to long-term strategic planning sets the stage for 5S to become an enduring cornerstone of operational excellence, driving continuous improvement and value creation.

The First Step To A Successful Operation

Case Studies: Successful Implementations of 5S

Introduction to Case Studies

The 5S methodology, derived from the Japanese words seiri, seiton, seiso, seiketsu, and shitsuke, represents a set of principles primarily focused on organizing a workspace for efficiency and effectiveness. Originating from lean manufacturing practices in Toyota's production system, 5S has evolved into a widely recognized tool for improving operational processes across various industries. The fundamental aspects of 5S involve sorting (seiri), setting in order (seiton), shining or cleanliness (seiso), standardizing (seiketsu), and sustaining discipline (shitsuke). These tenets are not only relevant to the physical work environment but also extend to digital and virtual spaces in today's technology-driven workplaces. Understanding the historical context and underlying philosophy of 5S provides a solid foundation for appreciating its significant impact on organizational performance and employee morale. As businesses continue to embrace continuous improvement methodologies, the integration of 5S practices is pivotal to achieving leaner, more efficient operations. By examining case studies, we can gain valuable insights into how 5S has been successfully implemented in diverse settings, demonstrating its adaptability and universal applicability in driving positive change.

Criteria for Selecting Case Studies

In selecting case studies for examination, it is imperative to establish a set of rigorous criteria to ensure that the chosen examples effectively illustrate the diverse applications and benefits of 5S methodology. The criteria for selection must encompass a range of industries, organizational sizes, geographical locations, and unique challenges faced during the implementation process. Consideration should also be given to the longevity of the 5S practices within the selected organizations, as long-term sustainability is a crucial indicator of success. Furthermore, the chosen case studies should encompass both successful implementations as well as instances where obstacles were encountered and overcome, providing a comprehensive understanding of the real-world dynamics of 5S adoption. It is essential to prioritize case studies that offer detailed insights into the strategies, methodologies, and tools utilized by the organizations to achieve notable results through 5S application. Additionally, the case studies must demonstrate a clear alignment between the

5S principles and the organization's overall objectives, showcasing how this methodology contributed to improving productivity, efficiency, safety, and employee engagement. Moreover, a comparative analysis of case studies from different sectors and regions can offer valuable perspectives on the adaptive nature of 5S and its capacity to drive operational excellence across varied contexts. Ultimately, the selection of case studies should aim to provide readers with a rich tapestry of experiences, enabling them to draw compelling lessons and best practices applicable to their own unique operational environments.

5S Implementation in Manufacturing Industries

In the context of manufacturing industries, the implementation of the 5S methodology plays a pivotal role in optimizing operational efficiency and overall productivity. This section delves into the significance of applying 5S principles within the manufacturing sector and explores the impact it has on various aspects of production processes.

The primary objective of 5S in manufacturing is to enhance workplace organization, streamline workflows, and minimize waste. By thoroughly sorting through tools, equipment, and materials, manufacturers can eliminate unnecessary items, thus freeing up space and reducing clutter. This process not only improves accessibility but also contributes to a safer work environment by eliminating potential hazards and obstructions.

Setting in order, the second step of 5S, involves assigning specific locations for each item and clearly labeling them. In a manufacturing setting, this step is fundamental in ensuring that all necessary tools and components are readily available at the point of use, thus reducing time wasted searching for items and minimizing disruptions to the production flow. Furthermore, a well-organized workspace enables employees to swiftly identify any missing tools or parts, leading to faster replenishment and reduced downtime.

The 'shine' phase emphasizes the importance of cleanliness and regular maintenance in a manufacturing environment. This involves establishing cleaning schedules and procedures to uphold equipment integrity and prevent malfunction due to dirt and debris accumulation. Additionally, a clean workspace fosters a sense of pride and respect among employees towards their work environment, ultimately influencing their overall mindset and dedication to maintaining high standards.

Standardizing practices and procedures across manufacturing operations enhances consistency and quality while bolstering overall efficiency. By implementing standardized work instructions, visual guides, and quality control checkpoints, organizations can ensure that each phase of the production process adheres to predetermined specifications and criteria. This equips teams with the knowledge and tools to consistently deliver high-quality outputs and reduces the likelihood of errors or defects.

Sustaining these improvements requires an ongoing commitment to the 5S principles. Regular audits, continuous improvement efforts, and employee training programs are essential for upholding the established standards and ensuring that the gains achieved through 5S implementation are perpetuated over time. This sustained dedication is integral to embedding the 5S philosophy within the organizational culture and reaping long-term benefits.

In conclusion, the integration of 5S principles within manufacturing industries brings about notable enhancements in productivity, safety, and quality. The structured approach of 5S not only optimizes operational processes but also cultivates a culture of excellence and continuous improvement within the manufacturing workplace.

Application of 5S in Service Sectors

In recent years, the principles of the 5S methodology have been increasingly adopted within service sectors to drive operational excellence and enhance customer satisfaction. Service organizations, such as healthcare facilities, financial institutions, hospitality industry, and administrative offices, have recognized the relevance and benefits of implementing 5S. The application of 5S in service sectors involves the systematic organization of workspaces, standardizing processes, and sustaining a culture of continuous improvement.

One key area of focus for service sectors when applying the 5S methodology is the 'Sort' phase, which involves eliminating unnecessary items and optimizing space utilization. In a healthcare setting, for example, the use of the 'Sort' principle can lead to organized supply rooms, reducing waste and ensuring that essential medical supplies are readily accessible for patient care.

The 'Set in Order' aspect of 5S is crucial in service sectors to streamline workflow and improve efficiency. Implementing visual management tools, such as color-coded filing systems in administrative offices or well-defined process flows in hospitality settings, can significantly enhance productivity and reduce errors in service delivery.

Furthermore, the 'Shine' component of 5S holds substantial importance in service sectors to maintain cleanliness and hygiene standards. This is particularly critical in healthcare facilities and hospitality establishments, where the cleanliness and orderliness of environments directly impact the well-being and satisfaction of patients and guests.

Standardizing practices through the 'Standardize' phase of 5S is pivotal for service sectors to ensure consistency and quality in service delivery. Establishing standardized protocols for customer interactions, financial transactions, or patient care processes contributes to enhanced reliability and customer trust.

Moreover, the 'Sustain' element of 5S is integral in service sectors to instill a culture of ongoing improvement and adherence to established standards. By nurturing a mindset of continuous improvement, service organizations can adapt to changing customer needs and market demands while maintaining high-quality service delivery.

In summary, the application of 5S in service sectors presents a transformative approach to enhancing operational efficiency, service quality, and overall customer satisfaction. Through the systematic implementation of the 5S principles, service organizations can achieve improved resource utilization, streamlined processes, and a heightened focus on delivering exceptional services.

Small Business Success Stories

In the realm of operational excellence, small businesses have displayed remarkable prowess in implementing 5S methodology to achieve outstanding results. These success stories serve as a beacon of inspiration and provide valuable insights into the practical application of 5S principles within small-scale enterprises.

One such exemplary success story originates from a family-owned manufacturing unit specializing in custom woodworking. By embracing the 5S approach, the company witnessed a transformative shift in its operational efficiency and overall work environment. Through the 'Sort' phase, redundant tools and equipment were identified and removed, streamlining the workflow and reducing clutter. 'Set in Order' not only organized the workspace but also enhanced accessibility to essential resources, leading to significant time savings during production. This meticulous approach also extended to 'Shine', where regular cleaning and maintenance routines resulted in a visually appealing and safer work environment.

Another narrative unfolds with a boutique consultancy firm that provides specialized services to diverse clientele. Implementing 5S principles enabled the business to optimize its resource allocation and increase client satisfaction. The team's diligent adherence to 'Standardize' procedures ensured consistent service delivery, while the 'Sustain' aspect maintained the high standards achieved. As a result, the consultancy firm not only improved internal processes but also demonstrated heightened professionalism to clients.

Beyond these specific instances, numerous similar accounts underscore how small businesses across various industries have harnessed the power of 5S to unlock their full potential. From independent retail outlets to neighborhood cafes, the systematic approach of 5S has encouraged a culture of excellence and continuous improvement, propelling these enterprises toward sustainable success.

Ultimately, these small business success stories reinforce the notion that the principles of 5S are universally applicable, transcending the scale of operations. They emphasize that, irrespective of size, any organization can reap the rewards of a well-structured and organized work environment, thereby enhancing productivity, quality, and ultimately, profitability.

Global Perspectives: 5S Across Continents

In our exploration of successful 5S implementations, it is imperative to gain insight into the global perspectives and varied applications of this methodology across different continents. The concept of 5S has transcended geographical boundaries and cultural differences, finding relevance and adoption in diverse industries and operational settings around the world. As we delve into the global landscape of 5S, it becomes evident that the principles of Sort, Set in Order, Shine, Standardize, and Sustain resonate universally, albeit with nuanced adaptations to local contexts.

Asia, particularly Japan, has been at the forefront of championing 5S practices, with its origins in Toyota's renowned Toyota Production System (TPS). The meticulous and systematic approach to workspace organization and efficiency has permeated manufacturing facilities across Asia, contributing to substantial improvements in productivity and quality. Moving to Europe, we encounter a similar commitment to 5S, where companies have integrated the methodology into their operations with a focus on lean principles and continuous improvement. The emphasis on standardized processes and visual management techniques has yielded impressive results, positioning 5S as an integral aspect of operational excellence in European industries.

Crossing the Atlantic to the American continent, we find a dynamic landscape of 5S implementation characterized by its integration into both manufacturing and service sectors. The adaptability of 5S tools and strategies has empowered organizations to streamline processes, reduce waste, and enhance workplace safety. Moreover, the emphasis on employee involvement and empowerment has been a hallmark of successful 5S initiatives in North and South America. As we explore the African and Australian continents, we witness the emerging adoption of 5S principles, driven by a growing recognition of the transformative impact of organized work environments and standardized practices.

The exchange of best practices and case studies from different continents offers invaluable insights into the adaptable nature of 5S and the multifaceted benefits gained through its implementation. Embracing the diverse global perspectives of 5S provides a rich tapestry of experiences and lessons learned, paving the way for cross-cultural collaboration and the continual evolution of operational excellence. By acknowledging the global reach and impact of 5S, organizations can leverage these insights to foster innovation, efficiency, and sustainable success in a rapidly evolving interconnected world.

Lessons Learned from Each Case Study

In analyzing the case studies presented, several crucial lessons can be gleaned from the successful implementations of 5S across various industries and geographical locations. Firstly, it is evident that a strong commitment from top management is paramount in driving the 5S initiative forward. Without the full support and involvement of leadership, sustaining the 5S practices becomes arduous. Additionally, the customization of 5S methodologies to fit the specific needs and nuances of different organizations emerged as a recurring theme. This adaptability showcases the flexibility of the 5S framework and its applicability across diverse settings. Moreover, the emphasis on employee involvement and empowerment was consistently highlighted as a driving force behind the successful implementation of 5S. Engaging employees at all levels fosters ownership of the process, leading to sustained improvements and a culture of continuous enhancement. Furthermore, the importance of rigorous training and ongoing education for employees cannot be overstated. The development of a shared understanding of 5S principles among all staff members is essential for the effective integration of these practices into daily operations. Another significant takeaway from the case studies is the need for clear communication channels and regular feedback mechanisms. Open dialogue facilitates the identification of obstacles and opportunities for refinement, ensuring that the 5S journey remains dynamic and responsive to evolving needs. Lastly, the consistent measurement and monitoring of key performance indicators were instrumental in gauging the impact of 5S implementations and recognizing areas for further enhancement. These key lessons underscore the integral components of successful 5S adoption and provide valuable insights for organizations embarking on their own operational excellence journeys.

Key Success Factors and Best Practices

Successfully implementing the 5S methodology requires a keen understanding of the key success factors and best practices that drive its effectiveness. In this section, we delve into the fundamental elements that set the stage for optimal outcomes in 5S implementation.

1. Leadership Commitment: The unwavering support and active involvement of leadership are pivotal in championing the 5S initiative. Leaders who visibly demonstrate their commitment to the process and actively participate in its execution set the tone for organizational buy-in and sustained efforts.

2. Employee Involvement and Empowerment: Engaging employees at all levels fosters a sense of ownership and accountability in the 5S journey. Empowering individuals to contribute ideas, take ownership of their workspaces, and participate in continuous improvement initiatives creates a culture of sustained excellence.

3. Comprehensive Training and Education: Equipping employees with the necessary knowledge and skills to understand and execute the 5S principles is essential. By providing targeted training programs and resources, organizations ensure that every team member comprehends the value of 5S and is capable of actively participating in its implementation.

4. Standardization and Visual Management: Establishing clear and standardized procedures, visual cues, and visual controls streamlines processes, enhances communication, and sustains the gains achieved through 5S. Visual management tools such as color-coded labels, signage, shadow boards, and visual displays play a critical role in maintaining organized and efficient work environments.

5. Continuous Improvement Culture: Embracing a culture of continuous improvement within the organization reinforces the ongoing application of 5S principles. Encouraging feedback, initiating regular audits, and recognizing and celebrating improvements contribute to an environment where 5S becomes ingrained in daily operations.

6. Flexibility and Adaptability: While adherence to established 5S principles is crucial, acknowledging the need for flexibility and adaptability allows for customization to meet specific organizational needs and evolving workplace requirements. Organizations that remain open to refining and adapting their 5S practices often realize greater returns and sustainability.

By prioritizing these key success factors and best practices, organizations can establish a solid foundation for successful 5S implementation and sustain a culture of operational excellence.

Long-term Benefits Observed

The implementation of 5S methodology has been associated with numerous long-term benefits across various industries and organizational settings. One of the primary long-term advantages observed is the sustained improvement in overall operational efficiency. By instilling a culture of continuous improvement and maintaining the 5S principles over time, organizations have experienced significant enhancements in productivity, reduced waste, and streamlined processes. This has translated into tangible cost savings and improved bottom-line performance.

Moreover, the commitment to 5S practices often leads to a safer and healthier work environment. Over time, the emphasis on cleanliness, organization, and standardized procedures contributes to a reduction in workplace accidents and incidents. As a result, companies that prioritize 5S not only enhance their productivity but also cultivate a culture of safety that aligns with regulatory requirements and mitigates potential risks.

Another long-term benefit observed is the positive impact on employee morale and engagement. Through the consistent application of 5S principles, employees feel empowered and take ownership of their workspace, leading to increased job satisfaction and motivation. This not only fosters a collaborative and cohesive work culture but also enhances overall employee retention, reducing training costs related to high turnover.

Furthermore, the systematic approach applied through 5S implementation facilitates better quality control and customer satisfaction in the long run. Standardizing workflows and ensuring the availability of necessary resources improves product and service consistency, resulting in higher customer trust and loyalty. Over time, this strengthens an organization's competitive position in the market and contributes to sustainable business growth.

From a strategic standpoint, the long-term benefits of 5S manifest in improved adaptability and resilience. By embedding lean principles through 5S, organizations develop a flexible operational framework capable of responding to changing market dynamics, technological advancements, and evolving customer demands. This adaptability ensures that businesses can withstand disruptions and remain agile in an increasingly competitive business landscape.

In summary, the long-term benefits of implementing 5S methodology encompass sustained operational efficiency, enhanced workplace safety, improved employee engagement, elevated product and service quality, and strategic resilience. These enduring advantages underscore the significance of 5S as a fundamental element in achieving organizational excellence and long-term success.

Conclusion and Future Implications

The 5S methodology has proven to be a transformative approach in improving organizational efficiency and productivity. As evidenced from the case studies presented, the long-term benefits of implementing 5S encompass various dimensions, including enhanced workplace safety, streamlined processes, reduced waste, and heightened employee morale. The culmination of these improvements leads to a sustainable competitive advantage for organizations that embrace and embed 5S principles into their operations.

Looking to the future, the implications of the widespread adoption of 5S are profound. With the continuous evolution of technology, the integration of digital tools and smart solutions into the 5S framework presents new avenues for optimizing workflows and data-driven decision-making. Additionally, as sustainability and environmental consciousness become increasingly crucial in business practices, 5S can serve as a catalyst for eco-friendly initiatives by reducing energy consumption, minimizing material waste, and promoting a greener operational footprint.

Furthermore, the global relevance of 5S underscores its potential to create standardized processes across diverse industries and geographical boundaries. As organizations increasingly operate on a global scale, the uniformity offered by 5S can facilitate seamless collaborations, supply chain efficiencies, and consistent quality standards.

In conclusion, the journey through the successful implementations of 5S exemplifies the transformative impact of this methodology. As we look ahead, it is imperative for businesses to recognize the enduring significance of 5S in driving operational excellence, adapting to emerging technological landscapes, and championing sustainable practices. By embracing the lessons learned from the case studies and aligning with future trends, organizations can position themselves at the forefront of innovation, resilience, and continual improvement.

The First Step To A Successful Operation

Overcoming Challenges in 5S Implementation

Identifying Common Obstacles

Implementing 5S methodology within an organization is a process that is not without its challenges. Identifying and understanding the common obstacles that can impede successful 5S adoption is crucial to developing effective strategies for overcoming them. One of the most typical roadblocks in 5S implementation is resistance to change. Many employees may be resistant to new processes and routines, often due to fear of the unknown or perceived threats to their established ways of working. Additionally, inadequate training and communication can pose significant obstacles as employees may not fully comprehend the benefits and rationale behind 5S. Another common obstacle lies in the lack of management support and leadership commitment. Without visible and consistent endorsement from upper management, employees may be less inclined to fully engage in the 5S efforts, leading to a lack of sustainability of the implemented changes. Moreover, a prevalent obstacle is the presence of ingrained habits and cultural norms within the organization that act as barriers to embracing the 5S principles. These habits and norms can manifest as resistance to discarding unnecessary items, maintaining cleanliness, or adhering to standardized procedures, all of which are fundamental to the success of 5S. In some cases, resource constraints and time pressures serve as significant obstacles to implementing 5S effectively. When organizations face competing priorities or limited resources, allocating the necessary time and investments towards 5S initiatives can become challenging. Furthermore, overlooking the need for continuous improvement and adaptation in the 5S journey can also be a major obstacle. Organizations that fail to recognize the dynamic nature of operational environments may encounter difficulties in sustaining the gains achieved through 5S, ultimately hindering long-term success. By proactively identifying these common obstacles and taking intentional steps to address them, organizations can better navigate the path to successful 5S adoption and realize the full benefits of this powerful methodology.

Cultivating Organizational Buy-In

In the pursuit of successful 5S implementation, one of the most pivotal yet challenging factors is cultivating strong organizational buy-in. Without the active support and engagement of key stakeholders, from leadership to front-line employees, the journey towards a streamlined and efficient workspace can face significant hurdles. Cultivating organizational buy-in involves a multifaceted approach that blends effective communication, fostering a sense of ownership, and aligning the 5S initiative with the overall strategic goals of the organization.

Effective communication lies at the heart of garnering support for any transformative endeavor. Leaders must clearly articulate the rationale behind implementing 5S, emphasizing its potential to enhance productivity, safety, and quality while reducing waste and inefficiencies. Moreover, the communication should extend beyond mere information dissemination; it should entail active listening and fostering open dialogue to address concerns and insights from employees at all levels. This inclusive approach fosters a sense of involvement and demonstrates the value placed on every individual's perspective.

Another critical element in cultivating buy-in is engendering a sense of ownership among the workforce. Employees are more likely to commit to the 5S methodology when they feel personally invested in its success. This can be achieved through involving them in the design and implementation of 5S initiatives, encouraging feedback, and recognizing and celebrating their contributions to the organization's improvement journey. Empowering employees to take ownership creates a culture of shared responsibility and accountability towards sustaining a clean, organized, and efficient work environment.

Aligning the 5S initiative with the broader strategic objectives of the organization reinforces its significance within the organizational framework. When employees understand how 5S directly contributes to achieving larger business goals such as improved customer satisfaction, operational excellence, and cost reduction, they are more likely to embrace and champion the initiative. This alignment necessitates a thorough understanding of the unique challenges and priorities within different functional areas or departments, allowing for tailored messaging and integration of 5S practices into existing workflows.

Ultimately, the cultivation of organizational buy-in demands a combination of persuasive communication, empowerment, and alignment with overarching business strategies. Successful implementation of 5S relies heavily on the collective commitment and enthusiasm of the entire organization, making the thorough cultivation of buy-in an indispensable precursor to sustainable transformation.

Tailoring Strategies to Fit Your Workplace

When it comes to implementing the 5S methodology within your organization, it is crucial to recognize that a one-size-fits-all approach may not yield optimum results. Tailoring strategies to fit your unique workplace environment is essential for successful implementation and sustained adherence to 5S principles. Tailoring strategies begins with a comprehensive assessment of your organization's specific needs, challenges, and existing processes. This involves gaining a deep understanding of the current workflow, workplace culture, and operational dynamics. By conducting thorough observational studies and engaging in open dialogue with employees at all levels, you can gain valuable insights into the areas that require improvement and the barriers that may impede successful implementation. Once the specific pain points and improvement opportunities are identified, it is imperative to develop customized action plans that align with the core principles of 5S while also accommodating the nuances of your workplace. This may involve adapting the terminology, tools, and visual cues used in the 5S methodology to resonate with your workforce and operational context. Additionally, tailoring strategies entail integrating 5S principles seamlessly into existing workflows and processes, without disrupting productivity or causing undue resistance. This often requires collaboration across departments and robust change management strategies to ensure a smooth transition. Furthermore, it is essential to consider the unique requirements of different work areas within your organization and customize 5S implementation plans accordingly. What works for the administrative office space may not necessarily be suitable for the manufacturing floor or the warehouse. Tailoring strategies should also encompass the allocation of resources, appropriate training programs, and continuous monitoring to ensure sustainable adherence to 5S practices. Finally, embedding a culture of continuous improvement is pivotal in tailoring strategies for long-term success. By fostering a mindset of ongoing refinement and adaptation, organizations can continuously tailor their 5S strategies to meet evolving needs and challenges. Ultimately, tailoring strategies to fit your workplace fosters ownership, engagement, and commitment among employees, leading to the successful integration of 5S principles into the organizational DNA.

Training and Development for Sustained Success

Training and development are integral components of sustained success in 5S implementation. It is imperative for organizations to invest in comprehensive training programs that equip employees at all levels with the knowledge and skills required to effectively engage in the 5S process. This chapter delves into the crucial aspects of training and development, exploring the strategies and best practices that foster a culture of continuous improvement within the organization.

Central to successful 5S implementation is the alignment of training programs with the specific needs and challenges of the workplace. Tailoring training content to address the distinct requirements of various departments and operational functions ensures that employees can readily apply 5S principles to their daily tasks. Through targeted training initiatives, employees gain a deep understanding of how 5S methodologies can optimize their work environments, leading to improved productivity, safety, and overall operational efficiency.

Furthermore, the development of internal champions and trainers plays a vital role in sustaining the momentum of 5S initiatives. Empowering select individuals within the organization to serve as advocates for 5S not only enhances knowledge dissemination but also encourages peer-to-peer learning and problem-solving. These internal champions can drive the culture of continuous improvement by regularly conducting refresher sessions, mentoring new employees, and championing 5S best practices throughout the organization.

In addition to initial training, ongoing development programs are essential for reinforcing 5S principles and fostering a commitment to long-term success. Continuous learning opportunities, workshops, and feedback mechanisms ensure that employees remain engaged and motivated in upholding the standards set forth by the 5S methodology. By nurturing a culture of learning and development, organizations can sustain the momentum of 5S implementation while adapting to evolving industry dynamics and technological advancements.

Ultimately, effective training and development programs serve as catalysts for cultural transformation within the organization. They instill a sense of ownership and accountability among employees, fostering a collective mindset focused on operational excellence. As organizational priorities shift and industry landscapes evolve, investing in robust training and development initiatives is fundamental to ensuring sustained success in implementing and upholding the 5S methodology.

Adapting 5S to Diverse Industries

In today's dynamic business environment, the principles of 5S methodology prove to be adaptable and beneficial across diverse industries. As organizations strive for operational excellence, the application of 5S principles extends beyond manufacturing and production settings to encompass sectors such as healthcare, education, service, and even technology. The key lies in understanding the unique characteristics and challenges of each industry and customizing the 5S approach to suit their specific needs.

Healthcare facilities, for instance, can utilize 5S to enhance patient safety, streamline processes, and reduce errors. By organizing medical supplies, optimizing storage space, and standardizing procedures, hospitals and clinics can achieve greater efficiency while prioritizing patient care. Similarly, educational institutions can employ 5S to create conducive learning environments, improve classroom management, and maximize resources.

Service-oriented businesses, including hospitality and retail, can benefit from 5S by fostering a clean and orderly atmosphere, ensuring quick access to necessary tools, and enhancing customer satisfaction through efficient service delivery. Meanwhile, in the technology sector, 5S principles can be tailored to software development, IT operations, and digital workflow management, contributing to streamlined processes and improved productivity.

The adaptability of 5S to diverse industries necessitates a thorough analysis of industry-specific requirements and a creative approach to tailoring the methodology accordingly. It involves engaging stakeholders from various departments, understanding their unique workflows, and collaborating to implement customized 5S strategies that address the specific pain points within each industry. Moreover, embracing diversity in 5S implementation allows for cross-industry knowledge transfer, enabling organizations to learn from best practices across different sectors and apply them innovatively.

Ultimately, the successful adaptation of 5S to diverse industries rests on the ability to recognize the common goal of operational efficiency while respecting the individual nuances of each sector. By acknowledging and leveraging the unique characteristics of different industries, organizations can harness the full potential of 5S methodology and drive continuous improvement and sustainable success across varied professional domains.

Integrating Technology Solutions

In today's dynamic and fast-paced business environment, the integration of technology solutions is paramount for successful 5S implementation across diverse industries. When considering the application of technology in the context of 5S, it is essential to explore how digital tools and systems can streamline processes, enhance communication, and ultimately support the principles of Sort, Set in Order, Shine, Standardize, and Sustain. One of the key aspects of integrating technology solutions into 5S initiatives is the utilization of digital platforms for organizing and visualizing workspace layouts and inventory management. Advanced software applications and digital mapping tools can aid in creating virtual layouts of work areas, facilitating efficient allocation of resources and minimizing waste. Furthermore, technology can play a crucial role in automating routine tasks, such as scheduling regular equipment maintenance, conducting digital audits, and tracking compliance with 5S standards. This automation not only improves accuracy and timeliness but also frees up valuable human resources to focus on higher-value activities essential for continuous improvement. Additionally, the incorporation of Internet of Things (IoT) devices and sensors enables real-time monitoring of equipment performance and environmental conditions, contributing to proactive maintenance and risk mitigation. Leveraging barcode scanning and RFID technology can enhance inventory control and material traceability, ensuring that items are easily locatable and properly stored. Virtual reality and augmented reality applications can be utilized for training employees on 5S principles, allowing for immersive simulations that depict optimal workspace organization and safety protocols. Moreover, digital communication channels and collaborative platforms facilitate effective sharing of best practices, insights, and improvement ideas among team members and departments. It is essential to note that the successful integration of technology solutions requires comprehensive training and change management strategies to ensure that employees are proficient in utilizing these tools and embrace their adoption. By effectively integrating technology solutions, organizations can advance their 5S initiatives, promote a culture of continuous improvement, and sustain operational excellence.

Fostering a Culture of Continuous Improvement

In an evolving business landscape, the pursuit of excellence is not a one-time event; it's a continuous journey. This chapter delves into the critical concept of fostering a culture of continuous improvement within the framework of 5S implementation. Developing such a culture goes beyond just the physical organization of the workspace; it involves nurturing a mindset that promotes ongoing reflection, innovation, and adaptability.

Central to fostering a culture of continuous improvement is the engagement of all employees at various levels within the organization, from frontline workers to upper management. Open channels of communication and a receptiveness to feedback are essential in empowering individuals to contribute their insights and take ownership of the improvement process. This inclusive approach cultivates a sense of shared responsibility and encourages employees to proactively seek out opportunities for enhancement.

Moreover, the integration of robust change management strategies plays a pivotal role in embedding a mindset of continuous improvement. It necessitates a thorough understanding of the human elements involved in change, addressing fears, uncertainties, and doubts that may arise. By effectively communicating the rationale behind changes and demonstrating empathy towards potential concerns, employees are more likely to embrace and champion improvements rather than resist them.

A culture of continuous improvement also thrives in an environment that emphasizes data-driven decision-making. Implementing systems for monitoring and measuring key performance indicators enables teams to identify areas for enhancement and assess the impact of implemented changes. This analytical approach provides valuable insights for making informed decisions, allowing the organization to adapt swiftly and effectively to dynamic market demands.

Furthermore, instilling the culture of continuous improvement often entails recognizing and celebrating successes, both big and small. Acknowledging and rewarding individual and collective efforts fosters a sense of achievement and motivates employees to sustain their commitment towards improvement initiatives. By highlighting and sharing success stories, the organization amplifies a culture of positivity and proactive engagement.

As organizations increasingly recognize the competitive advantages offered by agile and adaptive work cultures, the commitment to continuous improvement becomes a strategic imperative. Embracing this ethos results in enhanced operational resilience, heightened employee morale, and sustained competitiveness in an ever-evolving marketplace. The journey toward cultivating a culture of continuous improvement is not without challenges, but the rewards for those who persevere are substantial and enduring.

Managing Resistance to Change

Managing resistance to change is an essential aspect of successful 5S implementation. When introducing the 5S methodology, it's common for employees to exhibit varying levels of resistance due to fear of the unknown, concerns about increased workloads, or skepticism about the benefits of change. As such, effective management of resistance is crucial to ensure a smooth transition and sustainable adoption of 5S principles.

To effectively manage resistance to change, it's vital for leaders and change agents to first understand the underlying causes of resistance within their organization. This may involve conducting employee surveys, holding focus groups, and actively listening to concerns raised by staff. By gaining insight into the specific reasons behind resistance, organizations can tailor their approach to address these concerns directly, thus creating a more receptive environment for change.

Furthermore, communication plays a pivotal role in managing resistance. Open and transparent dialogue with employees can help dispel misconceptions and clarify the benefits of implementing 5S. Leaders should clearly articulate the rationale behind the change, outlining how it aligns with the organization's overall objectives and how it will ultimately benefit everyone involved. Building a compelling case for change can mitigate apprehensions and build support among employees.

Additionally, involving employees in the change process can significantly diminish resistance. Empowering staff to contribute ideas, provide feedback, and participate in decision-making fosters a sense of ownership and commitment to the changes being introduced. Moreover, providing thorough training and support to employees is imperative. Equipping them with the necessary skills and tools to adapt to the new processes instills confidence and minimizes resistance due to uncertainty or lack of proficiency.

Resistance to change can also emanate from a fear of the unknown. In such instances, offering visibility into the anticipated outcomes through pilot programs or gradual rollouts can alleviate apprehensions and allow employees to witness the benefits firsthand. Engaging champions or advocates of change within the organization can also help sway the opinion of hesitant individuals by showcasing successes and positive transformations resulting from 5S implementation.

Ultimately, managing resistance to change requires patience, empathy, and persistence. It necessitates constant reinforcement of the vision, consistent engagement with employees, and a willingness to address concerns as they arise. By prioritizing the human element in the change process and actively addressing resistance, organizations can foster a more inclusive and supportive environment that facilitates successful 5S implementation.

Leveraging Expert Guidance and Resources

In the pursuit of overcoming challenges in 5S implementation, organizations often find themselves in need of expert guidance and resources to navigate the complexities inherent in this process. Leveraging the knowledge and experience of industry experts, consultants, and trainers can significantly enhance the effectiveness of 5S initiatives. These professionals bring a wealth of practical insights, best practices, and tailored solutions that can address specific hurdles faced during implementation. By engaging with such experts, organizations can tap into a deep reservoir of knowledge and receive personalized guidance on customizing 5S methodologies to suit their unique operational contexts. Moreover, these experts can often provide valuable resources such as training materials, templates, and case studies that further facilitate the successful application of 5S principles. Collaborating with external consultants or subject matter experts also allows for an objective assessment of current processes and offers recommendations for improvement, contributing to a holistic approach to 5S implementation. In addition, resources such as online forums, industry publications, and professional associations can serve as valuable sources of support and information, enabling practitioners to stay abreast of the latest developments and proven strategies in the field of operational efficiency. Furthermore, leveraging internal expertise by identifying and empowering 5S champions within the organization can augment the effectiveness of 5S initiatives. These individuals can serve as internal ambassadors for change, driving enthusiasm and commitment among their peers while also serving as points of contact for sharing knowledge and troubleshooting challenges. By harnessing external guidance and internal talent, organizations can fortify their efforts to surmount obstacles in 5S implementation and foster a culture of continuous improvement that underpins sustained success.

Establishing Metrics for Overcoming Barriers

In the pursuit of implementing the 5S methodology, it is crucial to establish clear and measurable metrics for overcoming barriers. This entails a comprehensive approach that focuses on assessing, monitoring, and addressing challenges through quantifiable indicators. By developing robust metrics, organizations can effectively evaluate their progress and adapt strategies to navigate impediments during the implementation process. The following are key areas to consider when establishing metrics for overcoming barriers in 5S implementation:

1. Quantifying Resistance: One essential metric involves quantifying the level of resistance encountered at various stages of the 5S implementation. This may include identifying the

frequency and nature of resistance, as well as measuring the impact on project timelines and overall productivity. By gathering data on resistance, organizations can proactively devise targeted interventions to address concerns and mitigate opposition.

2. Compliance Rates: Tracking compliance rates with 5S practices and standards is vital for assessing the effectiveness of implementation efforts. Metrics related to compliance can encompass adherence to sorting and organizing principles, cleanliness standards, visual management, and sustaining newly established processes. Analyzing compliance rates provides valuable insights into the extent to which employees embrace and consistently follow 5S guidelines, allowing for corrective actions to be taken as needed.

3. Error Reduction and Efficiency Gains: Another crucial aspect of establishing metrics involves measuring error reduction and efficiency gains resulting from 5S implementation. Organizations can quantify improvements in quality, productivity, and operational efficiency by comparing pre-implementation error rates and performance indicators with post-implementation data. This empirical evidence not only validates the impact of 5S on business outcomes but also facilitates informed decision-making and resource allocation.

4. Employee Engagement and Feedback: Metrics for overcoming barriers should encompass measures of employee engagement and feedback. This includes gauging the participation levels in 5S activities, soliciting feedback on challenges faced, and evaluating the effectiveness of communication channels within the organization. By capturing the voice of employees, organizations can identify pain points and opportunities for improvement, ultimately fostering a culture of continuous dialogue and responsiveness.

5. Sustainability Index: Assessing the sustainability of 5S practices is fundamental for evaluating long-term success. Establishing a sustainability index involves evaluating the longevity and consistency of 5S implementation, including the durability of changes made, the integration of 5S into daily operations, and the cultural shift toward continuous improvement. Developing a sustainability index enables organizations to measure the enduring impact of 5S and strategize for ongoing improvement initiatives.

In conclusion, the establishment of metrics for overcoming barriers in 5S implementation is indispensable for steering organizations toward successful adoption of the methodology. By embracing a data-driven approach, organizations can pinpoint areas of improvement, optimize resources, and chart a course toward sustained operational excellence.

The First Step To A Successful Operation

Measuring the Impact of 5S on Productivity

Introduction to Productivity Metrics

In today's competitive business landscape, the assessment of productivity metrics plays a pivotal role in determining an organization's operational efficiency and overall success. By quantifying the output relative to the input, productivity metrics provide valuable insights into the utilization of resources and the effectiveness of processes. One widely used metric is labor productivity, which measures the output per employee, offering a clear indication of workforce performance and efficiency. Similarly, machine utilization and equipment effectiveness are vital metrics in manufacturing and production environments, enabling companies to optimize asset deployment and minimize downtime. Additionally, sales per square foot and revenue per employee are crucial productivity indicators for retail and service industries, illustrating the revenue-generating capacity per unit area and per team member, respectively. Furthermore, the measure of customer satisfaction and retention rates serves as an essential metric in assessing the effectiveness of customer relationship management strategies. Notably, these metrics not only reflect current performance but also serve as benchmarks for continuous improvement initiatives. As such, organizations utilize a combination of these metrics to evaluate their competitive positioning and identify areas for enhancement. Ultimately, a thorough understanding of productivity metrics empowers businesses to make informed decisions, streamline operations, and achieve sustainable growth.

Quantitative Insights: Key Performance Indicators

Key performance indicators (KPIs) serve as critical tools in assessing the impact of 5S methodology on productivity within an organizational setting. This section delves into the significance, selection, and application of KPIs in evaluating the tangible outcomes of 5S implementation.

When identifying KPIs, it is paramount to align them with the primary objectives of 5S, which include enhancing efficiency, reducing waste, and optimizing resource utilization. Common KPI categories encompass productivity metrics such as cycle time, lead time, and throughput. Additionally, quality-related KPIs like defect rates and rework percentage offer insights into the efficacy of 5S practices in elevating operational standards.

Moreover, financial KPIs play a pivotal role in quantifying the impact of 5S on cost savings, revenue generation, and overall profitability. These may comprise metrics related to inventory turnover, labor utilization, and utilization of facilities. By integrating these financial indicators with operational KPIs, a comprehensive picture of the bottom-line benefits derived from 5S adherence can be constructed.

Accurate data collection is integral to the reliability and relevance of KPIs. Leveraging advanced technologies, such as IoT sensors or automated data capture systems, ensures real-time tracking of relevant metrics and minimizes manual errors. Furthermore, standardizing data collection processes across various functional areas facilitates consistent and comparable KPI analyses.

Interpreting KPI trends involves not only analyzing the current state but also forecasting future performance trajectories. Trend analysis aids in identifying patterns of improvement or deterioration, enabling proactive measures to sustain gains or rectify deficiencies in 5S compliance. It fosters a data-driven approach to continuous improvement and augments the predictive capacity for evolving operational demands.

The amalgamation of diverse KPIs generates a composite index that encapsulates the multidimensional impact of 5S on productivity. This composite index serves as a holistic yardstick for gauging the success of 5S initiatives and provides a succinct representation of the cumulative effects across various facets of organizational operations. Emphasis should be placed on continually refining this composite index to reflect the evolving dynamics of the business environment.

In summary, the effective selection and utilization of key performance indicators are indispensable in quantifying the influence of 5S on productivity. By integrating quantitative insights garnered from KPIs, organizations can ascertain the extent of improvements attributable to 5S interventions and steer strategic decisions towards sustained operational excellence.

Qualitative Assessments: Employee and Stakeholder Feedback

Employee and stakeholder feedback is a crucial component of evaluating the impact of 5S on productivity. While quantitative data provides numerical insights, the qualitative assessments offer a more nuanced understanding of the human aspect of organizational change. In this section, we will explore the various methods for gathering and analyzing employee and stakeholder feedback in the context of 5S implementation.

Engaging with employees at all levels of the organization is essential to gain insights into their experiences with the 5S methodology. Conducting structured interviews, focus group discussions, and anonymous surveys can help capture the diverse perspectives and experiences related to the changes brought about by 5S. Encouraging open dialogue and providing a safe space for sharing concerns and suggestions is paramount to ensure the authenticity of the feedback received.

Furthermore, stakeholder feedback, including input from management, customers, and partners, can provide valuable external viewpoints on the effectiveness of 5S in enhancing overall productivity and quality standards. Interviews with key stakeholders and regular feedback sessions can uncover overarching themes and specific success stories that highlight the impact of 5S beyond the internal organizational dynamics.

When analyzing the qualitative feedback, it's important to look for recurring themes and patterns that shed light on areas of improvement, potential challenges, and notable successes. Thematic analysis and sentiment analysis can be applied to categorize and interpret the qualitative data, allowing for a deeper understanding of the emotional and perceptual aspects surrounding 5S implementation. By integrating the qualitative insights with quantitative metrics, a comprehensive picture of the 5S impact on productivity can be developed.

Moreover, creating a feedback loop where the findings from employee and stakeholder assessments are shared transparently fosters a culture of continuous improvement and inclusivity. Acknowledging the feedback received and showcasing how it informs decision-making processes demonstrates a commitment to organizational learning and development.

In summary, the qualitative assessments obtained from employees and stakeholders play a pivotal role in complementing the quantitative data, providing a holistic view of the impact of 5S on productivity. Incorporating diverse voices and narratives into the evaluation process enriches the understanding of the human dimensions of change and helps in shaping future strategies for sustaining and enhancing the benefits of 5S within the organization.

Data Collection Strategies for Accurate Measurement

In order to comprehensively assess the impact of 5S on productivity, it is crucial to employ robust data collection strategies that yield accurate and reliable measurements. The selection of appropriate data collection methods is fundamental to ensure the validity and integrity of the findings. Multiple sources of data, both quantitative and qualitative, should be considered to provide a holistic understanding of the changes brought about by the 5S implementation. One of the key data collection strategies involves establishing clear and measurable performance indicators aligned with the specific goals and objectives set during the initial stages of the 5S journey. These metrics could include but are not limited to, process cycle times, defect rates, inventory turnover, and equipment downtime. Additionally, implementing surveys, interviews, and focus groups can facilitate the gathering of qualitative insights from employees and stakeholders regarding their experiences and perceptions of the 5S initiative. Rigorous documentation of these qualitative inputs is essential for capturing the human aspect of organizational change and its potential influence on productivity. Leveraging technology plays a pivotal role in enhancing data collection accuracy. Automated systems, such as sensors, RFID tags, and software applications, provide real-time data on various operational parameters, offering unparalleled visibility into process efficiency and resource utilization. Moreover, the integration of data analytics tools enables the interpretation of complex datasets, allowing for predictive analysis and trend identification. However, it is imperative to strike a balance between technological sophistication and practical feasibility, ensuring that the chosen data collection methods align with the organizational context and capabilities. Ensuring the reliability and consistency of collected data necessitates the establishment of standardized protocols and procedures. Clear guidelines for data recording, storage, and retrieval should be communicated across the organization to minimize discrepancies and errors. Regular training sessions on data collection processes can further enhance the adherence to these protocols and promote a culture of data-driven decision-making. Lastly, periodic reviews and audits of the data collection framework should be conducted to identify areas for improvement and adaptation in response to evolving business requirements and industry trends. By implementing robust data collection strategies, organizations can effectively measure the impact of 5S on productivity, paving the way for informed decision-making and continuous improvement initiatives.

Analyzing Pre- and Post-Implementation Data Trends

Upon the successful implementation of the 5S methodology, it becomes imperative to delve into the thorough analysis of pre- and post-implementation data trends to fully comprehend the impact on productivity. By meticulously examining the data collected before the initiation of 5S practices and subsequently comparing it with the data gathered after the implementation, organizations can gain valuable insights into the tangible improvements brought about by 5S. Utilizing various statistical tools and analytical techniques, such as trend analysis, variance analysis, and correlation studies, allows for a comprehensive understanding of the changes in productivity metrics. This detailed analysis facilitates the identification of patterns, anomalies, and correlations, revealing the precise influence of 5S on productivity. As the data analysis unfolds, it is essential to contemplate not only quantitative aspects but also qualitative factors that may have contributed to the observed trends. Understanding the holistic impact of 5S involves integrating both numerical measurements and qualitative feedback from employees and stakeholders, providing a comprehensive perspective on the transformation in productivity. Leveraging these insights enables organizations to form informed decisions and strategies based on the nuanced data trends emerging from the implementation of 5S. Moreover, this analysis serves as an invaluable tool in gauging the effectiveness of the 5S methodology in different operational areas, shedding light on its varied impacts across diverse functions within an organization. Consequently, the meticulous examination of pre- and post-implementation data trends holds the potential to validate the efficacy of 5S in enhancing productivity, thus reinforcing its status as a pivotal operational strategy.

Case Study Analysis: Real-World Application of Metrics

In this section, we will delve into compelling case studies that exemplify the real-world application of metrics in assessing the impact of 5S on productivity. The case studies selected showcase diverse industries and operational settings, providing valuable insights into the practical implications of 5S implementation. Each case study will systematically examine the pre-implementation state, identifying inefficiencies, waste, and challenges within the workspace. This analysis is crucial in establishing a baseline for performance measurement. Subsequently, we will explore the specific 5S interventions introduced and the corresponding post-implementation data trends. These comprehensive evaluations aim to quantify the tangible improvements in productivity, efficiency, and workplace organization resulting from the implementation of 5S principles. Additionally, we will highlight the qualitative aspects, such as employee satisfaction, safety enhancements, and overall cultural transformation within the organizations. By presenting these detailed case studies, readers will gain a profound understanding of how 5S methodologies translate into measurable gains across a spectrum of industries. Moreover, insights from these real-world applications will equip practitioners with actionable strategies and best practices for implementing and measuring the impact of 5S on productivity within their own organizational contexts.

Impact Assessment: Translating 5S into Measurable Gains

In the context of organizational efficiency and productivity, the impact assessment of 5S methodology plays a pivotal role in determining the tangible benefits derived from its implementation. It involves a comprehensive evaluation of how the principles of 5S have translated into measurable gains across various operational aspects. This includes but is not limited to improvements in productivity, reduction in waste, enhanced safety standards, and streamlined processes.

Undertaking an impact assessment begins with establishing clear benchmarks against which the outcomes of 5S adoption can be measured. These benchmarks serve as reference points for evaluating changes in key performance indicators (KPIs) such as production output, lead times, error rates, and overall equipment effectiveness (OEE). By comparing pre-implementation data with post-implementation results, organizations can quantify the positive impact of 5S on their operational efficiency.

Furthermore, qualitative assessments play a significant role in capturing the non-quantifiable benefits of 5S. These encompass employee and stakeholder feedback regarding improved work environment, job satisfaction, and collaboration. Additionally, the impact assessment encompasses the alignment of 5S metrics with broader organizational goals, allowing stakeholders to understand how 5S contributes to strategic objectives.

Case studies provide valuable insights into how 5S practices have directly influenced specific business scenarios. Through detailed analysis of these real-world applications, organizations can gain a deeper understanding of the cause-and-effect relationship between 5S implementation and operational improvements. Moreover, this analysis serves as a reference point for other businesses looking to integrate 5S principles into their operations.

The impact assessment also involves identifying areas where technology can be leveraged to enhance measurement precision. This includes the utilization of advanced data capture tools, IoT devices for real-time monitoring, and software solutions for data analysis. Through the integration of technology, organizations can obtain more accurate and timely insights into the impacts of 5S on their productivity and overall performance.

Ultimately, the impact assessment allows organizations to concretely demonstrate the value of 5S methodology through empirical evidence. It forms the basis for informed decision-making, continuous improvement initiatives, and the strategic allocation of resources to sustain the benefits accrued from 5S implementation.

Leveraging Technology for Enhanced Measurement Precision

In today's fast-paced business environment, the role of technology in enhancing measurement precision cannot be overstated. The implementation of 5S methodology has facilitated a paradigm shift in the way organizations approach workspace optimization and productivity enhancement. Leveraging technology offers immense potential to elevate the accuracy and efficiency of measuring the impact of 5S on productivity.

One of the key technological advancements that have greatly contributed to enhanced measurement precision is the utilization of digital tools and software applications. These tools enable real-time data collection, analysis, and reporting, providing a comprehensive view of the 5S implementation's effects on productivity metrics. Automated data gathering eliminates human error and ensures consistent and reliable measurement, thereby offering a clear insight into the actual gains achieved through 5S adoption.

Furthermore, the integration of IoT (Internet of Things) devices within the workplace environment presents a revolutionary opportunity for precise monitoring and measurement.

Smart sensors embedded in workstations, storage areas, and production equipment can capture relevant data points related to workflow efficiency, resource utilization, and throughput. This real-time data streaming allows for deep insights into how 5S principles are impacting operational productivity at a granular level, fostering informed decision-making and targeted improvements.

Moreover, the emergence of advanced analytics and machine learning technologies empowers organizations to harness the full potential of their operational data. By employing sophisticated algorithms and predictive models, businesses can identify correlations, patterns, and trends that may not be immediately apparent through traditional measurement approaches. This allows for proactive problem-solving and the identification of opportunities for further optimization, thereby maximizing the benefits derived from 5S implementation.

The adoption of cloud-based platforms for storing and analyzing productivity data offers unparalleled flexibility and scalability. Cloud computing provides the infrastructure necessary for processing vast amounts of data efficiently, enabling organizations to handle large datasets with ease. Moreover, cloud-based solutions facilitate cross-functional collaboration and knowledge sharing, ensuring that key stakeholders across departments have access to real-time performance metrics and insights, driving a unified approach towards continuous improvement.

Overall, harnessing technology for enhanced measurement precision aligns with the ethos of 5S methodology, promoting a data-driven and strategically focused approach to productivity enhancement. By embracing these technological advancements, organizations can unlock the full potential of 5S implementation, making informed decisions backed by accurate and comprehensive data, thus propelling continuous improvement and sustainable productivity gains.

Addressing Challenges in Data Interpretation

Data interpretation is a critical aspect of any productivity measurement process, especially when evaluating the impact of methodologies such as 5S. However, it is important to acknowledge that there are several challenges associated with interpreting the data gathered during the evaluation of 5S initiatives.

One of the primary challenges in data interpretation is ensuring the accuracy and reliability of the data collected. Without accurate and reliable data, any interpretation will be flawed and may lead to misguided conclusions. This challenge can be addressed by implementing robust data collection processes, utilizing advanced technologies for data capture, and training personnel on effective data recording methods.

Another significant challenge in data interpretation lies in the complexity of correlating 5S implementation with specific productivity metrics. While it may be relatively straightforward to measure raw productivity metrics such as output per hour, linking these directly to 5S practices requires careful consideration of numerous influencing factors. Overcoming this challenge involves employing sophisticated analytical techniques, conducting thorough statistical analyses, and seeking expert guidance when establishing correlations between 5S and productivity metrics.

Furthermore, variations in the interpretation of qualitative data pose an additional hurdle when evaluating the impact of 5S on productivity. Qualitative data often involves subjective assessments and feedback from employees, which can introduce bias or inconsistency in interpretation. To address this challenge, it is essential to establish clear criteria for interpreting qualitative data and provide comprehensive training to interpreters to ensure uniformity and reliability in the analysis.

In addition to these challenges, navigating the sheer volume of data generated in a comprehensive productivity evaluation requires careful consideration. The process of sorting through, organizing, and synthesizing large datasets can be overwhelming and time-consuming. Implementing efficient data management strategies, including the use of data visualization tools and database management systems, can significantly mitigate this challenge and facilitate more streamlined data interpretation.

Finally, communication of findings and recommendations based on data interpretation represents a critical challenge. Effectively conveying complex data-driven insights to diverse stakeholders, including operational teams, management, and external collaborators, necessitates clear and concise reporting formats. Overcoming this challenge involves honing effective communication skills, adopting appropriate visualization techniques, and tailoring the message to resonate with each stakeholder group.

Addressing these challenges in data interpretation is imperative to derive accurate, meaningful insights into the impact of 5S on productivity, ultimately supporting informed decision-making and continuous improvement within operational environments.

Summary of Findings and Strategic Recommendations

As we conclude our exploration into the measurement of 5S impact on productivity, it becomes paramount to consolidate our findings and propose strategic recommendations for organizations aspiring to embrace the 5S methodology. The analysis of data interpretation challenges has highlighted the critical need for precise and accurate measurement techniques in order to effectively gauge the influence of 5S on productivity. Our thorough review of quantitative and qualitative metrics has facilitated a comprehensive understanding of the multifaceted nature of productivity and operational efficiency. We have observed that while quantitative indicators such as cycle time reductions, defect rates, and inventory turnover provide tangible insights, qualitative assessments derived from employee and stakeholder feedback offer invaluable perspectives on cultural shifts and morale improvements. One of the pivotal revelations gleaned through case study analysis is the direct correlation between successful 5S implementation and enhanced workplace safety, employee satisfaction, and customer satisfaction. Moreover, the integration of advanced technology for measurement purposes emerges as an instrumental element, enabling organizations to capture nuanced productivity enhancements with greater precision and granularity. However, it is imperative to acknowledge the challenges inherent in data interpretation, particularly in distinguishing between causal relationships and correlative observations within complex organizational ecosystems. Hence, the process of discerning true 5S impact demands rigorous scrutiny and analytical acumen. In light of these discoveries, we advocate for the development of tailored 5S performance scorecards that amalgamate both quantitative and qualitative metrics, providing a holistic assessment framework. These scorecards should be periodically reviewed and refined to align with evolving organizational objectives and market dynamics. Furthermore, strategic recommendations encompass the cultivation of a culture of continuous improvement, where 5S principles are ingrained into the fabric of daily operations. This necessitates robust training programs, leadership commitment, and participatory engagement at all levels of the organization. As organizations strive to harness the transformative potential of 5S, they must demonstrate a steadfast dedication to sustaining gains and fostering an environment of innovation. Additionally, cross-functional collaboration and knowledge sharing should be fostered to propagate best practices and drive collective ownership of productivity enhancement initiatives. Finally, embracing change management methodologies will be pivotal in effecting seamless 5S integration and mitigating resistance. It is through the culmination of these strategic imperatives that organizations can proactively steer towards operational excellence and enduring competitive advantage in today's dynamic business landscape.

The First Step To A Successful Operation

Future Trends and Innovations in Operational Efficiency

Introduction to Emerging Technologies

Advancements in technology have always played a pivotal role in transforming operational efficiency across various industries. This section explores the latest technological advancements that are set to revolutionize operational efficiency across industries. The continuous evolution and integration of emerging technologies such as artificial intelligence, big data analytics, Internet of Things (IoT), and automation are reshaping the ways in which organizations streamline their processes and enhance productivity. A comprehensive understanding of these technologies is crucial for businesses aiming to stay ahead in an increasingly competitive global landscape. By embracing these emerging technologies, businesses can optimize decision-making processes, drive innovation, and adapt to dynamic market demands. Furthermore, they can gain significant insights from data-driven approaches, enabling the identification of potential bottlenecks, prediction of maintenance needs, and optimization of resource allocation. Leveraging these technologies opens new opportunities for predictive and prescriptive analysis, empowering organizations with the ability to anticipate disruptions and make proactive strategic adjustments. Moreover, the advancements in technologies related to sustainability and workforce management are also shaping the future of operational efficiency. Energy-efficient solutions, sustainable manufacturing practices, and green technologies are becoming integral components of modern operational strategies. Furthermore, innovative workforce management tools and techniques are fostering a more agile and adaptable workforce, essential in today's rapidly changing business environment. Through this exploration of emerging technologies, businesses can gain valuable insights into the potential impact on operational efficiency and prepare themselves to harness these innovations effectively.

The Role of Artificial Intelligence in Operational Efficiency

Artificial Intelligence (AI) has emerged as a transformative force in the realm of operational efficiency, revolutionizing the ways in which businesses optimize their processes. AI encompasses a wide range of technologies that enable machines to perform tasks that typically require human intelligence, such as learning, problem-solving, and decision-making. In the context of operational efficiency, AI offers unprecedented opportunities to automate repetitive tasks, analyze complex data sets, and make real-time adjustments, thus driving productivity and cost-effectiveness. One of the key applications of AI in operational efficiency is predictive maintenance, wherein machine learning algorithms can analyze equipment performance data to forecast potential breakdowns, enabling proactive maintenance and minimizing downtime. Additionally, AI-powered systems can enhance demand forecasting accuracy, inventory management, and supply chain optimization, leading to streamlined operations and improved resource utilization.

Moreover, AI facilitates adaptive learning within operational environments, continuously optimizing processes based on changing parameters and variables. Through advanced analytics and cognitive computing, AI can identify patterns, anomalies, and correlations in operational data that may remain undetected by traditional analysis methods, thereby uncovering valuable insights for process refinement and performance enhancement. Furthermore, AI-driven robotics and autonomous systems have the potential to revolutionize production lines and logistics, increasing precision, speed, and safety while reducing reliance on manual labor.

Another notable aspect of AI in operational efficiency is its role in fostering intelligent decision support systems. By leveraging machine learning and natural language processing capabilities, AI can assist managers and frontline workers in making informed decisions, identifying optimization opportunities, and addressing operational challenges more effectively. This empowers organizations to implement data-driven strategies and adapt swiftly to dynamic market conditions, ultimately bolstering operational resilience and competitiveness.

Furthermore, the integration of AI with emerging technologies such as IoT and big data analytics presents new frontiers for operational excellence. AI-driven insights derived from interconnected devices and massive data streams can drive proactive maintenance, energy efficiency, and smart resource allocation, paving the way for agile and sustainable operations. As AI continues to evolve, it will likely play an increasingly pivotal role in shaping the future of operational efficiency, offering novel solutions and capabilities that redefine industry standards and elevate organizational performance.

Harnessing the Power of Big Data Analytics

The integration of big data analytics into operational practices has revolutionized the way organizations approach decision-making and process optimization. With the exponential growth of data in today's digital age, businesses are leveraging advanced analytics tools to extract actionable insights from large datasets. Big data analytics enables companies to uncover patterns, trends, and correlations that were previously obscured, empowering them to make informed strategic decisions. By harnessing the power of big data, organizations can gain a deeper understanding of their operations, customer behavior, market dynamics, and internal processes. This enhanced visibility allows for proactive problem-solving, efficient resource allocation, and improved risk management. Moreover, big data analytics facilitates predictive modeling and forecasting, enabling businesses to anticipate market trends, identify potential bottlenecks, and optimize production schedules. Through the analysis of historical and real-time data, organizations can enhance operational efficiency, reduce waste, and drive continuous improvement initiatives. The application of big data analytics extends beyond traditional operational functions and encompasses various aspects of business, including supply chain management, inventory optimization, and demand forecasting. Furthermore, the insights derived from big data analytics can fuel innovation and support agile decision-making processes, thereby fostering a culture of adaptability and responsiveness within organizations. However, it is essential for businesses to address the challenges associated with big data, such as data quality, privacy concerns, and technological infrastructure. Additionally, organizations must prioritize data security and compliance with regulatory frameworks to mitigate potential risks associated with the utilization of sensitive information. As big data analytics continues to evolve, it is imperative for businesses to cultivate a data-driven mindset and invest in the development of analytical capabilities. Embracing big data analytics as a core component of operational strategies empowers organizations to stay ahead of the competition, drive sustainable growth, and adapt to dynamic market conditions.

The Rise of Automation: Opportunities and Challenges

Automation, with its promise of enhanced efficiency and productivity, has emerged as a critical trend shaping the future of operational processes across industries. As organizations seek to streamline and optimize their operations, the integration of automated technologies presents both opportunities and challenges that deserve careful consideration.

Opportunities:

1. Enhanced Efficiency: Automation holds the potential to significantly increase operational efficiencies by reducing manual intervention and minimizing human error. Through the use of robotics and intelligent systems, tasks can be performed with greater speed and accuracy, leading to streamlined processes and cost savings.

2. Improved Safety: In environments where repetitive or hazardous tasks are prevalent, automation offers the opportunity to enhance workplace safety by minimizing the exposure of human workers to potential risks. By delegating such tasks to automated systems, the likelihood of workplace accidents and injuries can be mitigated.

3. Scalability and Flexibility: Automated systems can adapt to variable demand and workload requirements, offering scalability and flexibility that traditional processes may struggle to achieve. This adaptability enables organizations to respond more effectively to

market changes and customer demands.

Challenges:

1. Workforce Impact: The widespread adoption of automation raises concerns about its potential impact on the workforce. As tasks become automated, there is a need for reskilling and upskilling the workforce to remain relevant in an increasingly automated environment. Organizations must also address the potential displacement of certain roles and the accompanying socio-economic implications.

2. Technological Integration: The seamless integration of automated technologies with existing infrastructure and processes can pose significant technical challenges. Compatibility issues, cybersecurity concerns, and the need for specialized expertise in managing and maintaining automated systems are areas that require careful attention.

3. Ethical Considerations: The ethical implications of automation, particularly in sensitive decision-making processes, necessitate thoughtful deliberation. Addressing questions around accountability, transparency, and the ethical use of automated systems is crucial in fostering trust and acceptance of automation.

As industries continue to embrace automation as a means to drive operational excellence, it is imperative for organizations to weigh the opportunities and challenges inherent in this transition. By strategically leveraging automation while proactively addressing its associated challenges, businesses can position themselves to thrive in an increasingly automated operational landscape.

Leveraging Internet of Things (IoT) for Enhanced Processes

The integration of Internet of Things (IoT) technologies into operational processes has ushered in a new era of efficiency and connectivity. With IoT, physical objects are embedded with sensors, software, and other technologies that enable them to collect and exchange data over the internet. This interconnected network of devices holds immense potential for revolutionizing operations across various industries.

In manufacturing, IoT facilitates the concept of smart factories by enabling seamless communication and coordination between machinery and systems. Through real-time monitoring and data-driven insights, IoT empowers predictive maintenance, reducing downtime and optimizing production schedules. Furthermore, IoT-enabled supply chain management enhances visibility and transparency, allowing for streamlined logistics and inventory control. The ability to track and trace products throughout the production and distribution processes can lead to cost savings and improved customer satisfaction.

Beyond manufacturing, IoT plays a pivotal role in facility management. Building automation systems integrated with IoT contribute to energy conservation, sustainability, and enhanced occupant comfort. Smart sensors and connected devices enable intelligent climate control, lighting management, and security monitoring. These advancements not only reduce operational costs but also contribute to environmental stewardship, aligning with the growing emphasis on corporate social responsibility.

In the realm of healthcare, IoT applications have the potential to revolutionize patient care and medical processes. Remote patient monitoring devices and wearable technologies can transmit real-time health data to healthcare providers, facilitating proactive interventions and personalized treatment plans. Additionally, IoT-enabled medical equipment and infrastructure enhance operational efficiency within healthcare facilities, ensuring optimal resource utilization and patient safety.

IoT's influence extends into agriculture, where precision farming leverages data from interconnected sensors and devices to optimize crop yields, conserve resources, and promote sustainable agricultural practices. Real-time weather monitoring, soil analysis, and automated irrigation systems driven by IoT technology empower farmers to make informed decisions, minimize waste, and maximize productivity.

As organizations continue to harness the potential of IoT, considerations related to data security, interoperability of devices, and scalability of infrastructure remain imperative. Collaborative efforts among industry stakeholders, policymakers, and technology developers are essential to address these challenges and establish robust frameworks for maximizing the benefits of IoT in operational processes.

Sustainability Trends in Manufacturing and Operations

As the global business landscape continues to evolve, sustainability has emerged as a pivotal factor in driving operational efficiency within manufacturing and operations. Organizations are increasingly recognizing the imperative of integrating sustainable practices into their processes to not only reduce environmental impact but also enhance resource utilization and long-term viability. This chapter delves into the key sustainability trends shaping the future of manufacturing and operational practices. One prominent trend is the shift towards renewable energy sources and eco-friendly technologies. Businesses are investing in solar, wind, and hydroelectric power solutions to minimize reliance on non-renewable resources and mitigate carbon emissions. Additionally, there is a growing emphasis on circular economy principles, which advocate for minimizing waste generation and maximizing the lifespan of products through efficient recycling and reutilization strategies. Another significant trend involves eco-conscious supply chain management, where companies are proactively engaging with suppliers to ensure ethical sourcing, reduce transportation-related emissions, and optimize packaging materials. Furthermore, the adoption of sustainable manufacturing processes, such as lean production and green design, is gaining traction as a means to minimize energy consumption and material waste while maintaining high productivity levels. Integrated waste management systems, including advanced recycling technologies and waste-to-energy solutions, are also becoming essential components of sustainable operations. Moreover, the concept of sustainable product lifecycle management is reshaping the way organizations approach product design, from utilizing biodegradable materials to prioritizing longevity and reparability. In alignment with these trends, many industry leaders are championing the implementation of robust sustainability metrics and reporting mechanisms to monitor and communicate their environmental performance. Overall, embracing sustainability in manufacturing and operations not only addresses ecological concerns but also aligns with the pursuit of cost efficiency, regulatory compliance, and positive brand image. By staying abreast of these sustainability trends and integrating them into their operational strategies, businesses can position themselves as responsible corporate citizens while cultivating resilient and future-ready operations.

Innovations in Workforce Management

Workforce management is undergoing a significant transformation driven by technological advancements and changing organizational dynamics. As companies navigate the complexities of a globalized economy and seek to optimize their operations, innovative approaches to managing the workforce have emerged. This section delves into the key trends and developments shaping the landscape of modern-day workforce management.

One of the primary innovations revolutionizing workforce management is the adoption of advanced analytics and predictive modeling. Organizations are leveraging sophisticated data-driven tools to make informed decisions about workforce planning, recruitment, and retention. By analyzing various internal and external factors, such as market demand, skills gap, and employee performance metrics, businesses can align their workforce strategy with evolving business needs.

Furthermore, the emergence of artificial intelligence (AI) and machine learning has redefined traditional HR practices. AI-powered systems can automate routine tasks, streamline candidate sourcing, and personalize training programs, thereby enhancing overall workforce productivity and satisfaction. Additionally, machine learning algorithms enable more accurate demand forecasting and skill assessment, enabling organizations to proactively address staffing requirements and skills development.

Another notable innovation in workforce management is the emphasis on collaborative technologies and remote work solutions. With the proliferation of digital communication platforms and virtual collaboration tools, companies are embracing flexible work arrangements and distributed teams. This shift not only expands access to global talent but also promotes a more inclusive and adaptable work culture. By implementing robust remote work policies and deploying secure, user-friendly technology infrastructures, organizations can effectively manage diverse teams while promoting work-life balance.

Moreover, the growing focus on holistic employee well-being has led to the integration of wellness initiatives and mental health support into workforce management strategies. Employers are recognizing the interconnectedness of physical and mental wellness with job performance and are implementing programs that prioritize employee health and resilience. From mindfulness workshops and ergonomic workstations to comprehensive healthcare benefits, organizations are investing in measures that promote a healthy, engaged, and resilient workforce.

In conclusion, the future of workforce management lies in leveraging cutting-edge technologies, nurturing a culture of adaptability, and prioritizing employee well-being. By embracing these innovations, organizations can optimize workforce performance, foster greater agility, and navigate the evolving demands of the global marketplace.

The Impact of Digital Twins on Process Optimization

Digital twins have emerged as a groundbreaking technology with the potential to revolutionize process optimization across various industries. A digital twin is a virtual replica of physical assets, processes, or systems that enables real-time monitoring, analysis, and simulation. This innovative concept allows organizations to gain deep insights into their operations, leading to enhanced efficiency, productivity, and cost savings.

One of the key advantages of digital twins is their ability to provide a comprehensive view of complex processes. By creating a digital twin of a manufacturing plant, for example, organizations can monitor equipment performance, analyze production workflows, and identify potential bottlenecks in real time. This level of visibility empowers decision-makers to make data-driven adjustments and improvements, ultimately maximizing operational output.

In the realm of process optimization, digital twins offer predictive capabilities that significantly impact performance. Through sophisticated modeling and simulation, organizations can anticipate potential issues before they occur, enabling proactive maintenance and resource allocation. This proactive approach minimizes downtime, reduces the likelihood of equipment failures, and ultimately contributes to a more resilient and efficient operational environment.

Furthermore, the integration of digital twins with advanced analytics and machine learning enables continuous optimization. By leveraging historical and real-time data, organizations can gain valuable insights into process patterns and trends. These insights allow for the refinement of operational parameters, the identification of opportunities for improvement, and the implementation of more effective strategies, all contributing to long-term optimization and competitiveness.

The impact of digital twins extends beyond traditional manufacturing and industrial contexts. In sectors such as healthcare, transportation, and infrastructure, the application of digital twins offers transformative benefits. For instance, in healthcare, digital twins of patient care processes can lead to improved treatment protocols, personalized care plans, and streamlined resource utilization.

As organizations strive for greater agility and responsiveness, digital twins serve as powerful tools for scenario planning and risk management. Whether simulating the impact of market fluctuations on production or optimizing supply chain logistics, digital twins enable informed decision-making in dynamic and uncertain environments.

In conclusion, the adoption of digital twins holds immense potential for process optimization in diverse operational settings. By embracing this innovative technology, organizations can drive continuous improvement, enhance resilience, and achieve sustainable competitive advantages in an ever-evolving landscape.

Adapting to Remote Work: Tools and Strategies

In an era characterized by rapid technological advancements and a shifting work landscape, the concept of remote work has gained significant prominence. Organizations are increasingly recognizing the benefits of offering employees the flexibility to work from various locations, leading to the rise of distributed teams and virtual collaboration. Adapting to remote work requires a strategic approach that encompasses both tools and strategies tailored for this unique operational model.

Embracing remote work entails deploying a suite of essential tools designed to facilitate seamless communication and collaboration among geographically dispersed team members. Video conferencing platforms such as Zoom, Microsoft Teams, and Slack have become indispensable in enabling real-time virtual meetings, fostering face-to-face interactions, and enhancing team connectivity. Additionally, project management software like Asana, Trello, and Basecamp empower remote teams to organize tasks, set priorities, and track progress in a cohesive manner, ensuring alignment towards overarching goals despite physical separation. Emphasizing cybersecurity measures, including secure VPN connections and encrypted communication channels, is paramount to safeguarding sensitive organizational data when operating remotely.

Strategies for effective remote work center on cultivating a culture of autonomy, accountability, and trust within the workforce. Establishing clear communication protocols and delineating expectations regarding work hours and deliverables can mitigate potential misunderstandings and discrepancies. Encouraging regular check-ins and virtual team-building activities fosters camaraderie and cohesion, mitigating the sense of isolation often associated with remote work. Moreover, promoting a results-oriented approach over time-centric supervision fosters a sense of empowerment and instills a heightened sense of responsibility among remote employees.

As remote work blurs the boundaries between professional and personal lives, prioritizing employee well-being is imperative. Organizations must prioritize mental health initiatives, provide resources for ergonomically sound home workstations, and encourage employees to maintain a healthy work-life balance. Furthermore, honoring diverse work styles and accommodating individual preferences in terms of schedule flexibility can yield higher levels of satisfaction and productivity among remote workers. Nurturing a supportive and inclusive virtual environment where everyone's voice is heard and respected is fundamental to fostering a cohesive remote work culture.

In essence, navigating the transition to remote work necessitates a multi-faceted approach encompassing purposeful utilization of technological tools, coupled with the cultivation of robust strategies geared towards maintaining productivity, engagement, and well-being in a distributed work setting. By embracing remote work with the right combination of tools and strategies, organizations can effectively harness its numerous benefits while driving sustained performance and success in an evolving operational landscape.

Concluding Insights: Preparing for Tomorrow's Operational Landscape

In conclusion, the future of operational efficiency is shaped by a dynamic interplay of technology, innovation, and evolving workforce dynamics. As organizations navigate the ever-changing landscape, it is imperative to adopt a proactive approach to remain competitive and resilient. Embracing remote work as a viable operational model presents both opportunities and challenges. Leveraging advanced communication and collaboration tools, such as project management platforms and virtual meeting solutions, enables geographically dispersed teams to seamlessly collaborate and drive productivity.

Furthermore, the integration of artificial intelligence (AI) and machine learning algorithms is revolutionizing process optimization. From predictive maintenance in manufacturing facilities to intelligent routing in logistics, AI-driven systems are poised to deliver substantial gains in operational efficiency. However, as automation proliferates, organizations must prioritize upskilling and reskilling initiatives to empower employees with the necessary competencies to complement these transformative technologies.

Additionally, the advent of digital twin technology offers a paradigm shift in operational oversight and management. By creating virtual replicas of physical assets and processes, organizations can gain unparalleled insights, optimize resource utilization, and preemptively address potential bottlenecks. This not only enhances operational resilience but also facilitates continuous improvement through data-driven decision-making.

Looking ahead, the embrace of sustainability as a core tenet of operational strategies is essential. From green supply chain practices to energy-efficient operations, integrating sustainable initiatives into the fabric of organizational culture not only aligns with societal expectations but also drives cost savings and resilience against environmental risks.

Moreover, the evolution of workforce management encompasses remote talent acquisition, digital onboarding procedures, and the fostering of a cohesive organizational culture despite geographical dispersion. Proactive investment in employee well-being and development fosters a loyal, high-performing workforce that is pivotal in driving operational excellence.

As organizations adapt to the transformative forces shaping the operational landscape, they must remain agile and receptive to change. Embracing the forthcoming trends and innovations demands strategic foresight, adaptability, and a commitment to continuous learning and improvement. By cultivating a culture of innovation, harnessing the power of cutting-edge technologies, and prioritizing the development of human capital, organizations can position themselves to thrive in the dynamic operational landscape of tomorrow.

www.ingramcontent.com/pod-product-compliance
Lightning Source LLC
Chambersburg PA
CBHW071056240526
45469CB00006BD/2319